"The important thing is not to stop questioning"

Albert Einstein
1879 - 1955

Humps
for
140 yards

John Summers
2012

John Summers

www.john-summers.com

TicketyBoo!
PUBLISHING!

Humps for 140 yards

First published in Great Britain by TicketyBoo Publishing in 2007

A CIP catalogue record for this book is available from the British Library.

ISBN: 978-0-9553888-1-1

Typesetting in Trebuchet. Design by Tim Woolgar at Hybrid
Printed and bound in Great Britain by CPI Bath Press

Acknowledgements

For helping me to turn a bit of fun into a publishable entity:

> Sue, Alex, Benji, Tim, Gary, Loz, Zoe, Charlie, Alison
> and Michael David Swan (desperate to see his full name here)

For providing the substance to fill these pages and the answers to my specific searching questions (also for giving permissions for appearances in this book though, where this has not been finalised, I will be pleased to give acknowledgements in the next edition):

> dependable Personal Assistants, tireless Customer Service departments
> and all others who have made useful contributions.

For helping to raise funds for ICAN:

> you readers who have actually parted with money for this book.

Foreword

We live in contemporary times. Confusing contemporary times. No previous civilisation has had as much information available to them. Yet today, blessed with an abundance of books, blogs and bytes, we often fail to make sense of any of it.

Well it's just not good enough. Despite all this data, we are still lacking answers to some of life's most fundamental questions. Or at least we were before I started writing. I've made it my mission to uncover answers to questions that others do not have the will to pursue. And now I am ready to share what I have learnt. Read on to find out things like:

-       How can you work for the church but take Sundays off?
-       Why are 'knickers' plural yet a bra is 'singular'?
-       Why is it forbidden to enter an electrical box in Ullapool?
-       When will the sign outside Mount Stewart school be metricated?
-       Where is the New War Office?

As if the answers to these questions are not important enough, I'm using this publication to raise money for charity. For each of the first 10,000 copies of this book sold (in hardback or softback), £1 will be donated to I CAN (Registered Charity Number 210031) to support their work in improving children's communications.

So, as well as having a laugh, you can help do some good.

John Summers

helps children
communicate

REGISTERED CHARITY 210031

Who is I CAN?
Registered Charity Number 210031

I CAN is the children's communication charity. They work to develop speech and language skills in all children, particularly those with a communication disability.

Communication is a foundation life skill. It affects our ability to learn, form relationships and make friends. Unable to share feelings and needs, children become frustrated and isolated. Indeed, there is a direct and proven link between communication disability and emotional/ behavioural problems.

In some parts of the UK, as many as half the children entering our primary schools do not have the speech and language skills needed to learn, make friends and achieve. One in ten children have a communication disability - that's 1.2 million in the UK. Without the right help, these children can be left behind.

What could £10,000 do for I CAN?

The extra funds generated by this book will help I CAN's specialist work. Specifically £10,000 could be used to:

- train 100 nursery teachers with the skills to provide extra support to young children with communications difficulties in the critical pre-school years.

- fund 50 school-age children, with severe communication difficulties, to spend a weekend at an I CAN Regional Centre where they will benefit from specialised support in order to build confidence.

How can I make an additional donation?

Please visit I CAN's website at www.ican.org.uk

Northwick Park Road, Harrow, Middlesex

Julian Alexander
Lucas Alexander Whitley Ltd
14 Vernon Street
London
W14 04J

24th September 2002

Re: "Summers' Questions"

Dear Julian

It's not every day that an idea to publish a book like this reaches your office (is it?) So please drop everything. And then brush your entire ensemble of desk-top furnishings to one side.

When your desk is clear, sit back. Breathe deeply. Imagine yourself at home in your favourite chair. Perhaps you're day dreaming. Perhaps you're dozing. Perhaps your faithful Labrador is dribbling a damp patch on your left leg.

Then someone comes into the room. Your wife? "Julian darling! You must look at this! It's outrageous. Someone has gone to the effort to ask all sorts of small-minded questions to all sorts of high-minded people. And the oddest thing is that they've actually bothered to reply to him. Take a look!"

That is your invitation to open your eyes and begin reading this manuscript. Enjoy!

When you have finished, please let me know whether now is the right time to crack open the celebratory champagne. I look forward to your comments.

Kind regards

John Summers

Writers' Agents

John Summers
Northwick Park Road
Harrow
Middlesex
HA1 2NY

2nd October 2002

Dear Mr Summers

Thanks so much for your letter and indeed the other letters.

To be honest I don't know whether you should crack open the champagne but I'm afraid it won't be with me as I just don't know how to do this project and so I'd better pass before you waste a glass of the finest on me.

With best wishes

Julian Alexander

Lucas Alexander Whitley Ltd

14 Vernon Street, London W14 ORJ

Telephone: 020 7471 7900   Fax: 020 7471 7910

Registered Office: 105 St. Peter's Street, St. Albans, Herts AL1 3EJ. Registered No. 3226762 VAT Reg. No. 678 1684 85

Edmunds Gardens, Booker, High Wycombe, Buckinghamshire

John Major
10 Downing Street
London
SW1A 2AA

5th January 1991

Dear John,

I am a bit confused by this democracy thing. If I write a letter to you (as I am doing now) then how can I know whether you will see it or not?

If you don't see it then who chooses whether you see it or not? Surely that's the person who's really running the country? How can this be democratic when this letter is addressed to you, not your 'doorkeeper'?

So, how many letters do you read each week and have you seen this letter yourself?

Kind regards

John Summers

Tony Blair
10 Downing Street
London
SW1A 2AA

2nd May 2002

Dear Tony,

I am a bit confused by this democracy thing. If I write a letter to you (as I am doing now) then how can I know whether you will see it or not?

If you don't see it then who chooses whether you see it or not? Surely that's the person who's really running the country? How can this be democratic when this letter is addressed to you, not your 'doorkeeper'?

So, how many letters do you read each week and have you seen this letter yourself?

Kind regards

John Summers

12

10 DOWNING STREET
LONDON SW1A 2AA

From the Correspondence Secretary

18 January 1991

Dear Mr Summers,

The Prime Minister has asked me to thank you for your recent letter and to explain that as he receives many thousands of letters each week, it is impossible for him to reply personally in each case.

Mr Major must, therefore, in the normal course of business, delegate to his staff and Government Departments the responsibili~ dealing with many of them.

Yours ~

Mr J Summers
Edmunds Gardens
Booker
High Wycombe
Buckinghamshire
HP12 4LP

10 DOWNING STREET
LONDON SW1A 2AA

7 June 2002

From the Direct Communications Unit

Mr John Summers
Northwick Park Road

Harrow
Middlesex
HA1 2NY

Dear Mr Summers

The Prime Minister has asked me to thank you for your letter of 2 May.

Mr Blair receives many thousands of letters each week and is not always possible for him to reply personally to the gre majority of them.

Yours sincerely

BEN GROVER

Different PMs, different parties, ~t same old replies...!"

Northwick Park Road, Harrow, Middlesex

Miss Christina Jansen
Councillor of Press and Cultural Affairs Department
Royal Netherlands Embassy
38 Hyde Park Gate
London
SW7 5DP

9th September 2002

Dear Miss Jansen

Congratulations! You have been selected to participate in the British Customer Responsiveness Survey, 2002.

Please can you answer this simple question? People from Poland are called Poles so why aren't people from Holland called Holes?

If you would like further information on the results of this important national survey then please let me know.

I look forward to hearing from you.

Kind regards

John Summers

Ambassade van het
Koninkrijk der Nederlanden

Mr John Summers
▉ Northwick Park Road
Harrow
Middlesex
HA1 2NY

Royal Netherlands Embassy
Press and Cultural Affairs
38 Hyde Park Gate
London SW7 5DP

Date	17 December 2002	*Processor*	Mignon Tenpierik
Our ref.		*Tel.*	▉
Page	1/1	*Fax*	+44 (0)20 7581 0053
Encl.		*E-mail*	▉
Subject	**The Netherlands!**		
C.c.			

Dear Mr Summer,

Herewith as requested information on the Netherlands for the British Customer
Responsiveness Survey 2002.

The information shows that Holland is only a part of the Netherlands. This explains
why we are not called Holes. Furthermore, attached some more details on our
language.

I hope the above information will be of assistance to you.

Yours sincerely,

Mignon Tenpierik
Public Information Officer

THE NETHERLANDS / HOLLAND

A question of correct idiom is whether one should say "Holland" or "The Netherlands". The
official name of the Kingdom is The Netherlands but the term Holland is often used. This
name originally belongs to the old County of Holland; roughly the area of the present
provinces of North and South Holland. As this area has been since the middle-ages,
economically and politically an important part of the country, its name became widely - but
wrongly - used for the whole of The Netherlands.

15

The Old Rectory, Devon

Sir David Attenborough
BBC Television Centre
White City
210 Wood Lane
London
W12 7TS

25th May 2006

Dear Sir David

Last night's 'Are We Changing Planet Earth?' was an excellent documentary on climate change. Well done.

It sparked a huge debate in our household. You put across many good points and showed how everyone can do something, irrespective of their level in society. Governments can legislate to put proper taxes on dirty things. And humble members of the public (like me!) can simply switch things off.

Here's where it gets tricky. You made a 2 part series. Wouldn't it have been better for the environment if you had condensed all your points into 1 programme and then, at the beginning of the next, simply said "Please switch off your TV for 1 hour." The effect of millions of people doing this would probably be enough to put several power stations out of action. Just think of all the tonnes of bad gas that would have been saved from the environment.

Did you think of this option? If not, what do you think about it now?

Kind regards

John Summers

Natural History Unit

22nd June 2006

Dear Mr Somners

Thank you for your letter commenting on the two recent programmes on climate change which I narrated. I am sorry not to have acknowledged it before now but I left to filming overseas before the second programme was transmitted, and have only recently returned to this country.

Several hundred letters awaited me. They are full of comments, arguments, suggestions and questions. Sadly it is simply not possible practical for me to address every point individually and at length, but I can assure you that I will consider them all most carefully.

Thank you again for having written.

Yours sincerely

David Attenborough

Northwick Park Road, Harrow, Middlesex

Sir John Stevens
Commissioner
Metropolitan Police
New Scotland Yard
Broadway
London
SW1H OBG

10th December 2002

Dear Sir John

Please stop me from doing something illegal.

You've probably heard about 'Jeans for Genes', the charity that raises thousands for research into genetic diseases affecting children.

What you may not have heard about is 'Bare for Bears', an event supporting the plight of the Alaskan Brown Bear. Some adventure companies charge people $15,775 to go and shoot these wonderful animals. Their clients see it as some sort of holiday.

I am planning to organise a sponsored walk. To empathise with the bears, I'll be doing it in the depths of our winter. And I'll be bare. Now this is the tricky bit. How bare can I go in public? I don't want your people laying their hands on my body! I will wear a leather-effect thong and was hoping to go topless. If I have to wear something up there, then the dark bits around my nipples (I think they are called areolae) are 36mm across. Please can you give me the minimum measurements that I can get away with?

I don't know if you are the man who knows the details but, if not, I'm sure you know the officer who does.

Kind regards

Jane Summers

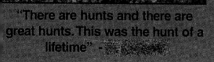

"There are hunts and there are great hunts. This was the hunt of a lifetime" -

METROPOLITAN POLICE

Working for a safer London

Ms Jane Summers
██ Northwick Park Road
Harrow
Middx
HA1 2NY

Malcolm Simpson
Superintendent
Public Order Branch
New Scotland Yard
Broadway
London
SW1

Telephone: 0207 230 ████
Facsimile: ████
e-mail:

www.met.police.uk

Your ref:
Our ref: TPHQ/598/02

27.12.02

Dear Ms Summers

Thank you for your letter of 10th December 2002 that has been passed to me from the Commissioner's office.

If you are planning a sponsored walk then you must contact the police in the area in which you intend to walk. They can advise you re the route and minimise any road safety or traffic problems that may result.

What you choose to wear on your walk is a matter for you, however if a complaint is made to police re your behaviour or attire then police may have to intervene to prevent a breach of the peace.

I cannot be more specific at this stage without further information.

Yours sincerely

Malcolm Simpson
Superintendent

Northwick Park Road, Harrow, Middlesex

Andy Matheson
Highland Council
Street Lighting Section
Craig Road
Dingwall
Rosshire
IV15 9LE

2nd September 2002

Dear Mr Matheson

I am an explorer.

I like to go places where no-one has been before. If I then discover that I have been pipped to the post, I like to be the first to publish that I have been to such and such a place.

Imagine my delight, then, when I saw a small metal box on Ullapool's high street with the sign "For permission to enter this pillar please telephone 0370 345 ███".

I have been pot-holing and down a 300 year old mineshaft. I have also been stuck in a cupboard. But I have never managed to get inside something as small as your metal box. Therefore I hope that you will give me permission to attempt to enter the box.

Back to my earlier point on the need to be the first to get somewhere vs the need to be first heard about getting somewhere, has anyone else managed to enter this box before me?

I look forward to a positive note from you as I have been told that you are "the man that knows".

Kind regards

John Summers

The Highland Council
Comhairle na Gaidhealtachd

SERVING Ross & Cromarty

Director of T.E.C. Services: Mrs M. McLauchlin

Your ref:
Our ref: ULL/100
Date: 10TH SEPTEMBER 2002

████ ,NORTHWICK PARK ROAD,
HARROW,
MIDDLESEX
HAI 2NY

Dear Mr. Summers,

Thank you for your letter of 2nd September 2002 regarding the lighting pillar you discovered in Ullapool.

The pillar is in fact an electrical supply pillar for controlling the streetlights in the area, and the permission to enter is only in relation to a third party entering the unit to undertake electrical work.

As you will understand, space is limited within the pillar because of the electrical equipment housed within it. Quite apart from that, it would dangerous for someone without the relevant electrical training to access the pillar.

To answer your last point, you would not be the first to enter the box – over the years dozens of electricians have worked here, so this is not virgin territory!

I hope you have enjoyed your stay in Ross-shire, and that this letter has not curbed your enthusiasm for undiscovered places.

Yours sincerely,

AREA LIGHTING ENGINEER
(ROSS AND CROMARTY DIVISION)

A. Matheson. **Area Lighting Engineer**. Ross and Cromarty Area
Lighting and Communications Section, T.E.C. Services
Craig Road Depot, Dingwall IV15 9LE Tel: (01349) 865263 Fax: (01349) 867293

The Old Rectory, Devon

Juliet Riccio
Customer Services Manager
Gossard
Units 1-4 Ridgeway Court
Grovebury Rd
Leighton Buzzard
Bedfordshire
LU7 4SF

17th May 2006

Dear Juliet

Help!

No-one else seems to know the answer to this question. But everyone says that you have an opinion. Please put an end to the hunting!

My question covers a slightly delicate matter. Take a look at the average woman. She has two, how can I put it, chest bumps and one, err, lower private area. So why do you recommend that a woman wears a bra and knickers? Surely it has to be a set of bras (for the two 'bumps') and a singular knicker (for the lower region)?

Please let me know that you will clear this up once and for all. Buying women's underwear is confusing enough for my husband, without this added layer of mystery and intrigue!

Kind regards

Jane Summers

Berlei

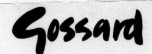

Units 1-4, Ridgeway Ct
Grovebury Road
Leighton Buzzard
Bedfordshire LU7 4SF
Telephone: 01525 851122
Fax: 01525 851007
www.gossard.com
www.berlei.com

Ref: MP/JS

19th May 2006

Mrs Jane Summers
The Old Rectory
▓▓▓▓▓▓▓▓
Devon
▓▓▓▓▓▓

Dear Mrs Summers

Thank your for your letter dated 17th May.

It does seem quite confusing that we use the word knickers rather than knicker, but I'm afraid I cannot give you an explanation for this. I think the word bra is a bit easier to explain as the full word should be Brassiere, over the years it has been shortened to bra.

I have looked up both words in the Cambridge Dictionary and they are described as follows: -

Knickers: - Plural noun
UK (US panties) a piece of underwear worn by women and girls covering the area between the waist and the tops of the legs:

Interestingly enough, there is not the word knicker in either the Cambridge or English dictionary, it is knickers in both.

Bra: - (FORMAL brassiere)
a piece of women's underwear that supports the breasts.

Sorry we are unable to help more on this occasion.

Yours sincerely

Mrs M Perry
Customer Services

Registered Office: DBApparel UK Ltd, Britannia Wharf, Monument Road, Woking, Surrey GU21 5LW. Registered in England Number 552438

The Old Rectory, Devon

Jeremy Pelczer
Managing Director
Thames Water Utilities Ltd
PO Box 3073
Swindon
SN38 8WY

One rule for us and another for them...

THAMES Water is under fire after high-pressure jets were used to wash its head office building in Reading — while its domestic customers are banned from using hosepipes.

22nd May 2006

Dear Jeremy

I know that you have a tough job to do what with catching all the water that falls on your patch, taking stuff out to protect the public from Legionnaire's disease, adding other stuff in to protect our teeth, then squirting it out to thousands of customers. That's not to mention clearing away tonnes of sewage that we dump down your drains. (Incidentally, how much sewage do you turn around each year?)

My main question is this. Given that we have hosepipe bans over much of the country, why oh why was it reported that your Reading head office building was washed with high-pressure jets? I just don't get it.

Please can you explain this to me?

Kind regards

John Summers

Customer Relations

Your ref	324363
Our ref	Suzanne Furkins
Name	08457 200897
Phone	01793 424291
Fax	Customer.Feedback
Email	@thameswater.co.uk

J Summers

he Old Rectory

Devon

31 May 2006

Hosepipe ban

Dear Mr Summers

Thank you for your letter of 22 May 2006 addressed to our Managing Director, Mr Jeremy Pelczer. Your letter has been passed to me for reply.

It's true that a building occupied by Thames Water staff was washed down using pressure hosepipes. A number of our staff occupy two rented floors of this building, although we do not own the block. We therefore cannot control what happens there, any more than we can control the cleaning of any other premises.

The use of these jet washes is infuriating. Some weeks ago, we decided not to wash the windows of our own premises, as we realise how important it is to set an example in the current drought.

The building concerned belongs to another company. However, we have expressed our views forcibly to the managing agent, but they have declined to stop the work, since it does not breach current restrictions

The hosepipe ban, which came into force on 3 April 2006, prohibits the use of a hosepipe or similar apparatus for the watering of a private garden or the washing of a private vehicle. Our power to impose this ban can be found under Section 76 of the Water Industry Act 1991.

We take the view that a private garden is one that the public does not have a right of access to; this may include communal gardens within residential estates or gardens within commercial boundaries.

A "private motor car" means any mechanically propelled vehicle intended or adapted for use on roads; other than public service or commercial goods vehicles.

As we can only work within current legislation, at this present time there is little we can do. Although this company is not in breach of the ban, we are asking all our customers to be sensible in their water usage.

Thames Water
PO Box 436
Swindon
SN38 1TU

T 08457 200897
F 01793 424291
I www.thameswateruk.co.uk

Thames Water Utilities Ltd
Registered in England and Wales
No. 2366661, Registered office
Clearwater Court, Vastern Road,
Reading, Berks RG1 8DB

Finally, to answer the specific question you raised regarding sewage. In our June return it shows we turned around 263,941 tonnes of dry solids.

I hope this helps to clarify the current restrictions, however, if you have any further queries please feel free to contact our Drought Line on 0845 641 ███. You may also like to visit www.beatthedrought.com for more information.

Yours sincerely

Suzanne Furkins
Customer Relations

Enc. The Thames Water quality promise leaflet

Northwick Park Road, Harrow, Middlesex

The Library
Office for National Statistics
Cardiff Road
Newport
NP10 8XG

11th June 2002

Dear Sir / Madam,

I wrote to you on April 29th but have not received a reply yet. You've probably been caught up with the Golden Jubilee and the World Cup like the rest of us!

Please will you provide me with the answer to the following questions:

1. How many enquiries does the Office for National Statistics receive a year?

2. How many of these enquiries ask "how many enquiries does the Office for National Statistics receive each year"?

While the next may seem an obscure trivial question, I would value your response.

3. What are the more obscure trivial questions that you have received?

4. In addition, now that I have not received a response from you within the 10 days stated in your charter, what percentage of your responses are sent out within 10 days?

Kind regards

John Summers

national
STaTiSTiCS

national
STaTiSTiCS

Office for National Statistics · Government Buildings · Cardiff Road · Newport
Gwent NP10 8XG · Tel: 01633 815696 · Fax: 01633 652747
E-mail: info@ons.gov.uk · www.statistics.gov.uk

National Statistics Customer
Enquiry Centre
Government Buildings
Cardiff Road
Newport
South Wales NP10 8XG
Tel: 0845 6013034
Fax: 01633 652747
Email: info@statistics.gov.uk

John Summers
Northwick Park Road
Harrow
Middx
HA1 2NY

Our ref: 104/2002

Your ref:

Date: 13/06/2002

Dear Mr Summers,

Public Enquiry

Thank you for your further letter dated 11 June 2002. I am sorry to hear that you have not received a reply to your original letter. However, I can confirm that a response was posted to you on 10 May 2002 (copy enclosed).

With regard to your further question I can inform you that all public enquiries handled by the Customer Enquiry Centre are responded to within ten days. However, on occasions detailed enquires are forwarded through to the appropriate business areas where response times may exceed ten days.

Yours sincerely,

Richard Wilton

Richard Wilton

Dear Mr Summers,

Public Enquiry

Thank you for your letter dated 29 April 2002. My response to your questions are as follows:

1. The National Statistics Customer Enquiry Centre (NSCEC) receives in excess of 40,000 public enquiries each year.

2. The NSCEC cannot recall receiving any other public enquiry which has asked this question over the past year.

3. Regrettably, we do not have the resources to identify the more obsure public enquiries which have been received.

Yours sincerely,

Richard Wilton

Northwick Park Road, Harrow, Middlesex

The Hon Russell Marshall CNZM
The High Commissioner to London
New Zealand High Commission
New Zealand House
80 Haymarket
London
SW1Y 4TQ

10th July 2002

Dear Mr Marshall

Please can you end the debate once and for all?

A much-traveled colleague of mine, Richard, insists that he is correct. He
believes that every time a new immigrant is accepted into New Zealand, the
local government has to increase the sheep quota by 23 in order to maintain
the balance between man and flock.

Is this really true or have I been spun a yarn? If not, what is the real ratio of
people to sheep back home?

Do you have any brochures giving an overview of the New Zealand wool
industry?

I look forward to hearing the truth from the man who knows!

Kind regards

John Summers

New Zealand Herald

Some of the 10 identical Fresian calves cloned from one adult cow by AgResearch Scientists, 1998.

Agriculture

...lture are major industries, providing a high proportion of New Zealand's export
...lly farming has centred on sheep and cattle to produce sheepmeat, beef, wool,
...ides, although since the 1970s new types of livestock have included deer and
...re grown mainly for the home market. Horticulture has always provided well for
...t since the 1970s horticultural produce has become an important export earner.
...eat and wool farming is mainly hill country and rolling downs. The lowlands and
...rt dairy, arable and horticultural production. Increasing use of coastal flat land
...been a major development over recent decades.

...rrent situation and trends

...e makes up more than half of New Zealand's merchandise exports. Uniquely,
...ped countries, New Zealand farmers are almost totally exposed to world market
...e no subsidies from government and have to compete with subsidised production
...s. However, the GATT Uruguay Round Agriculture Agreement began to take
...Agreement imposes progressive reductions on the subsidies that other countries
...ural production and exports. One effect is to increase access opportunities for
...ts into overseas markets.

How many farms?

In 1901 there were 62,786 farms occupying 14 million hectares. Total stock numbers were 1.2 million cattle, 20 million sheep, 251,000 pigs and 266,000 horses.

In 1996 there were 66,045 farms covering 16.5 million hectares. Stock numbers were 4.2 million dairy cattle, 4.8 million beef cattle, 47.4 million sheep, 424,000 pigs, 1.2 million deer and 228,000 goats.

Source: Statistics New Zealand.

Population 3.714 million in 1996

...BY FARM TYPE, AS AT 30 JUNE 1996

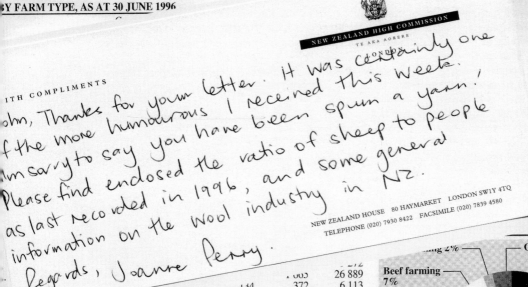

NEW ZEALAND HIGH COMMISSION
TE AKA AORERE
LONDON

...ITH COMPLIMENTS

...ohn, Thanks for your letter. It was certainly one
...f the more humourous I received this week.
...m sorry to say you have been spun a yarn!
Please find enclosed the ratio of sheep to people
as last recorded in 1996, and some general
information on the wool industry in NZ.
Regards, Joanne Perry.

NEW ZEALAND HOUSE 80 HAYMARKET LONDON SW1Y 4TQ
TELEPHONE (020) 7930 8422 FACSIMILE (020) 7839 4580

					26 889
			154	372	6 113
		..s	197	469	5 671
	10 433	4 288	..s	..s	17 157
708	2 368	2 553	..s	..s	5 570
...er seed					
1 640	..s	2 671	..s	..s	13 493
...owing ...	..s	..s	89	..s	644

...ng 2%

Other farming and idle land 4%

Beef farming 7%

Mixed livestock 3%

Dairy farming 12%

Sheep - beef cattle 15%

Northwick Park Road, Harrow, Middlesex

Dr George Carey
The Archbishop of Canterbury
Lambeth Palace
London
SE1 7JU

4th July 2002

Dear Dr Carey

For many years I have been thinking about whether to pursue a following in the church. Indeed, recently, I have been inspired by the words of a number of the clergy. And I believe that I too could be an inspirational leader within the church. (Certainly this is what my mother has always told me.)

Talking to people on the street, it seems that the church appears to have less relevance to society today. However I think that now is the time to show how it has much more relevance than these people imagine!

I know that we all live in contemporary times and, indeed, this puts many pressures on the fragile family unit. We seem to be pulled in all directions at once. Furthermore, it seems that the more labour-saving devices we invent (by 'we' I mean the scientific community – I am most definitely not an inventor), the busier we become. Oh for the life before mobile phones and internet connections! But I digress.

Here is my issue – the thing that is holding me back from leaping head-first into ecclesiastical training (I've managed to get over the first hurdle – that of having to spell the damned word). How can I lead the flock seven days a week yet also stay true to my family values? How can I possibly work on Sundays, especially as the Good Lord declared it a day of rest? Would it be feasible to be a vicar on a 9 to 5 contract, plus overtime for emergencies?

Please can you advise me how to work through this conundrum? In addition, what is the best way to begin my journey to a life 'in the cloth'?

Kind regards

John Summers

LAMBETH PALACE

Mr John Summers
█████ Northwick Park Road
Harrow
Middlesex
HA1 2NY

The Revd Canon Dr David Marshall
Chaplain to the Archbishop of Canterbury

9 July 2002

Dear Mr Summers

Thank you very much for your letter dated 4 July to the Archbishop, to which, in his absence, I am replying on his behalf.

The simple answer to your many very interesting questions about the implications of 'leaping head-first into ecclesiastical training' (many congratulations indeed on spelling it correctly!) is that you ought in the first instance to approach the clergyman appointed in your part of London diocese to advise all those considering this path. In your case, the clergyman you need to contact is The Revd Trevor Mapstone whose contact details are as follows:

The Revd Trevor Mapstone
Director of Ordinands
██ ████████ Park Road
Harrow
Middlesex
██████

Tel: ████████████

I am sure that if you contact Mr Mapstone he will be able to answer your questions very helpfully.

Yours sincerely

David Marshall

The Old Rectory, Devon

Customer Service Department
Waitrose Limited
Doncastle Road
Bracknell
Berkshire
RG12 8YA

25th May 2006

Dear Sir or Madam

I see that you have started to sell tomotoes on the vine. I assume that this is another way that you can boost your profits by getting me to do all the work of pulling them off the vine. Therefore please will you reduce the price to reflect the cost of my labour? I don't come cheap, you know! However I'm prepared to price myself out at the minimum wage which, for workers aged 22 and over, is £5.05 an hour.

I've timed myself taking the tomatoes out of the plastic packet, pulling them off the vine then getting out those fiddly green bits that the vine left behind. Then I had to put the plastic packaging in the bin and the vine and fiddly bits in my composter bin. All this took me 29 seconds. And that works out at just over 4p of my time. So, please reduce the price of your tomatoes on the vine by at least 4p immediately.

By the way, what exactly is an 'ocado'? I know that it's some sort of exotic vegefruit but it's not listed in my dictionary.

Kind regards

John Summers

BY APPOINTMENT TO
HER MAJESTY THE QUEEN
GROCERS AND
WINE & SPIRIT MERCHANTS
WAITROSE LIMITED BRACKNELL

BY APPOINTMENT TO THE LATE
HER MAJESTY QUEEN ELIZABETH
THE QUEEN MOTHER
GROCERS
WAITROSE LIMITED BRACKNELL

Waitrose

Mr J Summers
The Old Rectory

Devon

8 June 2006
1-7814830-7

Dear Mr Summers

Thank you for your letter of 26 May 2006.

With reference to your comments on the cost and time involved in preparing tomatoes sold on the vine, I wish to point out that there are alternative tomatoes available to buy at Waitrose that are not still on the vine for those customers who prefer them this way. Tomatoes on the vine sell very well, a lot of customers preferring to buy them, but we do offer the choice.

I have to say that I am not aware of a fruit or vegetable known as an 'ocado'! However I do of course know of the company called Ocado who offer an internet grocery shopping delivery service supplying Waitrose goods. Perhaps this may be the Ocado you have heard of?

Finally, I would like to thank you for taking the trouble to write. I can assure you of our continued commitment to providing you with the best possible standards of merchandise and service at Waitrose.

Yours sincerely

J Sheppard (Mrs)
Customer Service

900 H/O

Food shops of the John Lewis Partnership

Customer Service

Bracknell, Berkshire RG12 8YA
Telephone 01344 825232
Facsimile 01344 824978
email customer_service@waitrose.co.uk
www.waitrose.com

Waitrose Limited, Registered in England 99405, Registered Office, 171 Victoria Street, London SW1E 5NN

The Old Rectory, Devon

Darren Shapland
Chief Financial Officer
J Sainsbury plc
33 Holborn
London
EC1N 2HT

13th June 2006

Dear Darren

I see that you have started to sell tomatoes on the vine. I assume that this is another way that you can boost your profits by getting me to do all the work of pulling them off the vine? Therefore please will you reduce the price to reflect the cost of my labour? I don't come cheap, you know! However I'm prepared to price myself out at the minimum wage which, for workers aged 22 and over, is £5.05 an hour.

I've timed myself taking the tomatoes out of the plastic packet, pulling them off the vine then getting out those fiddly green bits that the vine left behind. Then I had to put the plastic packaging in the bin and the vine and fiddly bits in my composter bin. All this took me 29 seconds. And that works out at just over 4p of my time.

Therefore please confirm that you will reduce the price of your tomatoes on the vine by at least 4p immediately.

Kind regards

John Summers

Sainsbury's

Our reference: 1-153039556/av/ab

06 July 2006

Mr John Summers
The Old Rectory

Devon

Sainsbury's Supermarkets Ltd
33 Holborn
London
EC1N 2HT

Telephone 020 7695 6000
Fax 020 7695 7610
www.sainsburys.co.uk

Dear Mr Summers

Thank you for writing to Darren Shapland, our Finance Director. Your letter has been passed on to me for a reply.

I am sorry that you have been inconvenienced by having to pull our tomatoes off the vine. I know how frustrating this can be, particularly when you are looking forward to tucking into some nice, juicy tomatoes. We offer them on the vine as this helps to preserve their great taste and unique aroma.

I can promise you that our prices truly reflect those that we pay to secure supply of the high quality products we know our customers expect. These tomatoes come from a very select group of growers, and the process of harvesting them with their vines is very difficult and labour intensive.

However, we know that some customers prefer their tomatoes to be loose, and we do offer many different varieties. I can particularly recommend our Taste the Difference Pomodorino tomatoes.

Thank you again for writing. I hope that you will find everything to your satisfaction on your next visit to Sainsbury's.

Yours sincerely

Alex Voskou
Executive Office

Registered office as above
Registered number 3261722 England
A subsidiary of J Sainsbury plc

100% post consumer waste recycled paper

20/001004

35

Northwick Park Road, Harrow, Middlesex

Professor Brian Rainford
Head of Department
Department of Physics and Astronomy
University of Southampton
Highfield
Southampton
SO17 1BJ

9th September 2002

Dear Professor Rainford

I am writing to you as one of the nation's leading physiscientists. After all, your department produced 2 out of the 3 finalists for the Best Physics Student in the 2002 SET awards. And you achieved the highest possible rating in the 2001 Research Assessment Exercise, making you one of the top five departments in the UK.

Please can you answer this simple question? How much faster would the speed of light be if lightning took a straight path down to earth rather than a haphazard zigzag? It's been keeping me awake at night. (The question, not the lightning.)

I look forward to hearing from you as I have been told that you are 'the man who knows' and I am looking forward to a good night's sleep.

Please can I have a reply at 'lightning speed'?

Kind regards

John Summers

University of Southampton

Department of Physics and Astronomy	University of Southampton
Professor B D Rainford	Highfield
~~Head of Department~~	Southampton
	SO17 1BJ
	United Kingdom

Telephone +44 (0)23 8059 2095
Fax +44 (0)23 8059 3910
Email bdr@phys.soton.ac.uk

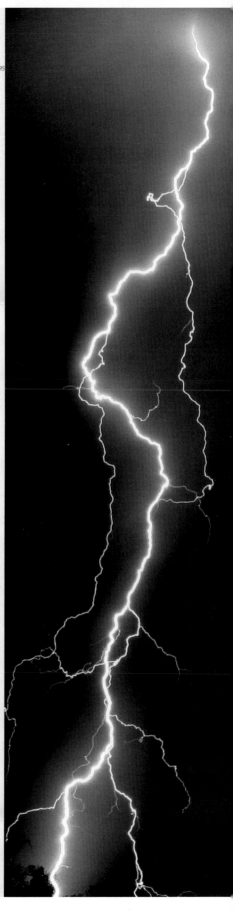

Mr John Summers,
Northwick Park Road
Harrow
Middlesex
HA1 2NY

Dear Mr Summers,

I do apologise for not getting around to replying to your query. I've just ended my stint as Head of Department, but found myself with a very heavy teaching load. So I haven't had much sleep either since last October.

I have a problem understanding your question, actually, so I can't provide you with a snappy answer. Also I have to admit that your question is outside the area of my immediate expertise. Anyway let me have a go......

What I don't understand about the question is the implication that lightning is actually caused by light travelling from the clouds to the earth. This is not the case. What appears to happen in a thunderstorm, is that very large electrical charges build up in the clouds. The electric fields they produce are large enough to ionise the air molecules, just as happens in a spark-plug in a petrol engine. Ionisation is a process where electrons are stripped off atoms, leaving free electrons and positively charged ions. The electrons thus released are propelled along the electric field gradient until they reach the ground. As a result of collisions between these accelerated electrons and the air molecules a column of air a few metres wide becomes ionised, allowing a huge electric current to flow between the clouds and the earth, thereby eliminating the potential difference between the earth and the cloud. This rapid flow of current causes intense local heating which produces a shockwave that we hear as thunder. The light we see as lightning is due to the excitation of molecules in the ionisation process. This is very similar to the process by which light is produced in a domestic fluorescent tube.

So the light we see in lightning is very much a secondary effect of the passage of the enormous electrical current produced by ionisation of the air. The reason for the haphazard zig-zag is that the path taken by the ionising electrons has a random element, depending on the local density of ion pairs.

I don't think it is worth losing sleep over, but lightning is a very complex phenomenon. I'm not sure what the speed of the lightning stroke is, but I would guess that overall it is much slower than the speed of light – after all there is first the phase

involving the development of the ionisation, followed by the flow of the current. The speed with which the current flows will depend on the mechanism for ionisation: if it depends entirely on electron collision, then it cannot be very fast, perhaps a million metres per second? This is about a hundred times slower than the speed of light! However one of my colleagues thinks that photo-ionisation is probably important, in which case the current pulse must happen at speeds approaching the speed of light.

As you have probably heard light travels in a vacuum at an ultimate speed – about 300 million metres per second. Einstein's theory of relativity shows that material bodies cannot travel faster than this speed. However when light travels in a medium, such as air, it actually slows down. You can see the effect of the slowing down in refraction effects, for example when you look at a stick half submerged in water it looks bent. This is because the light travelling in the water has a much lower speed than when it emerges into the air: so the wave-fronts get bent at the water-air interface. There have been some remarkable recent experiments on a special form of matter called a Bose condensate that show that when light travels in this medium it can be slowed down to a few kilometres per hour – walking pace! None of this effects Einstein's predictions, however.

I hope this helps. If you have access to the web, you might try browsing the topic of lightning. If I come across anything authoritative, I'll let you know.

Best wishes and happy Xmas

Yours,

Brian Rainford

Brian Rainford

Northwick Park Road, Harrow, Middlesex

The Marketing Director
CadburyTreborBasset (UK)
Denham Way
Maple Cross
Herts
WD3 9XB

8th January 2003

Dear Sir / Madam

'CadburyTreborBasset' – that's a bit of a mouthful, isn't it!? I've got chocolate
and liquorice all mixed up together and I'm not sure I like it.

Anyway, on to my point. I hope you had a happy Christmas. I did. Complete
with all the trimmings. But imagine my surprise when, before decorations
came down on 12th night, I saw posters advertising your Easter Creme Eggs! I
have checked my diary, to make sure that I haven't missed something, and I'm
reassured to see that Easter Day is not until April 20th. So, please can we have
a breather between the Chocolate Bumper Selection Pack of Christmas and the
Creme Egg of Easter?

In particular I would like to know how the original Cadbury brothers, who
founded your company along strict Quaker lines in 1899, would react to the
fact that you have started Easter so early? Why have their current descendents
thrown away their original values?

Also I have seen that Tesco are selling Hot Cross Buns now. However they have
never claimed to be founded upon philanthropic principles. Are you just
copying them?

I am concerned about the blurring of our seasons and events in order to satisfy
the appetites of companies like Cadbury and Tesco. If we have next year's
Easter being promoted before this year's Christmas then I won't know where I
am in the year! Am I a lone voice on this issue?

Kind regards

Jane Summers

Jane Summers

"CHOCOLATE & A HALF"

CADBURY LTD.

PO BOX 12
BOURNVILLE
BIRMINGHAM B30 2LU
CONSUMER DIRECT LINE 0121-451 4444
SWITCHBOARD TELEPHONE 0121-458 2000
FAX No. 0121-451 4297
http://www.cadbury.co.uk

12 February 2003

Ms J Summers
████ Northwick Park Road
HARROW
Middlesex
HA1 2NY

Our Ref:- 0945527A

Dear Ms Summers,

Thank you for your letter of 8th January which has just arrived on my desk.

In answer to your query that originally after their launch in 1923 Cadbury's Creme Egg ere sold as an Easter only product for many years. Now they have been available as a product for the whole Spring season. This is in response to demands both from our consumers and customers, who see Cadbury's Creme Egg as a symbol of the new season - the Spring season.

I totally agree that we should not mix our seasons and our firm recommendation to our customers is not to display then until after the Christmas season has finished.

Thank you for taking the time and trouble to write to us.

Yours sincerely

Peter Creighton
Cadbury Limited

Registered In England. Company Number 155256   Reg Office: PO Box 12, Bournville B'ham B30 2LU

INVESTOR IN PEOPLE

39

Our Ref: 5081484

14 January 2003

TESCO

Customer Service
PO Box 73
Baird Avenue
Dryburgh Industrial Estate
Dundee
DD2 3TN
Freephone   0800 505555

Ms Jane Summers
▓ Northwick Park Road
HARROW
Middlesex
HA1 2NY

Dear Ms Summers

Thank you for your recent letter and seasons greetings.

I was very sorry to hear of your disappointment with our early marketing of Easter products.

I would like to explain that these products are very popular with our customers and, especially, with their children. Over the last few years we have received much feedback about the products that our customers want to buy at this time of year. Nevertheless, it would not be our intention to cause any offence with our advertising or with the products on sale. I can confirm that your comments have been passed onto our marketing department so that they may be aware of your views.

Thank you for taking the time and trouble to write to us. We are always pleased to have comments and suggestions from our customers as, with your help, we can further improve our services, products and facilities.

Yours sincerely
For and on behalf of Tesco Stores Ltd

Geraldine Martin
Customer Service Manager

Tesco Stores Ltd. (519500). Company Registered in England. Registered Office: Tesco House, Delamare Road, Cheshunt, Waltham Cross, Hertfordshire EN8 9SL

LAMBETH PALACE

Mr John Summers
▮ Northwick Park Road
Harrow
Middlesex
HA1 2NY

Mr Andrew Nunn
Lay Assistant to
The Archbishop of Canterbury

21 January 2003

Dear Mr Summers

The Archbishop of Canterbury has asked me to write thanking you for your 8 January letter about Cadbury's Cream Eggs and Tescos Hot Cross Buns. Since neither chocolate eggs nor hot cross buns have any spiritual or indeed liturgical significance I am afraid the Archbishop must admit to having no standing in when Tesco's sell them. Like you I regret the passing of discernible seasons in such things. Many people might however think that there were more important things to worry about – not least at a time when this country might be about to go to war.

With very best wishes

Northwick Park Road, Harrow, Middlesex

Sir Edward George
Governor
The Bank of England
Threadneedle Street
London
EC2R 8AH

11th June 2002

Dear Sir Edward

I have just received one of those new £5 notes that were mentioned on the radio recently. To me it looks just like one of the millions that you are calling back in.

Please can you tell me if this is one of the forgeries? And how can I tell if, for instance, a lady in Tesco's gives me £5, whether it is OK or a forgery?

Finally is it true that Sven-Goran Eriksson will be the first foreigner on the new £50 note if England win the World Cup?

Kind regards

John Summers

Enc: £5 (HB68 978942)

You can continue to use the old style £5 and £10 banknotes until they are ~~withdrawn~~ from circulation.

You can contin~~ue~~
with the
until it

~~det~~ails of other

BANK OF ENGLAND
CUSTOMER BANKING AND NOTES DIVISION

Threadneedle Street
Note Issue Policy Office (BB-3)
London EC2R 8AH

Tel: 020 7601 ▮▮▮
Fax: 020 7601 ▮▮▮
Ref: NIP/Corres/17871/SJH

18 June 2002

John Summers
▮▮ Northwick Park Road
Harrow
Middlesex
HA1 2NY

Dear Mr Summers

Thank you for your letter of 11 June, which you sent to the Governor and which has been passed to this office for reply.

I can confirm that your £5 note is genuine and is returned within. I also enclose a copy of the leaflet describing the new £5 note and our "Know Your Banknotes" leaflet which has been produced specifically to assist people to identify the security features incorporated within each note.

The Bank has celebrated eminent British personalities on the reverse of our banknotes since 1970. The character chosen must have made an indisputable contribute to their particular field, and we also need to have access to sufficient material on which to base a design.

The Bank has no intentions at present to introduce a new £50 note.

I hope this letter has been of assistance to you.

Yours sincerely

Alan Sheppard
Manager

~~Ba~~nk of England, Threadneedle Street, London EC2~~R~~ ~~...nformation;~~
~~...601 4012~~
~~...kofengland.co.uk~~
~~...fengland.co.uk~~
~~...es, Bank of Englan~~~~d~~
Threadneedl~~e...~~ London EC2R 8AH

~~For~~ further information visit the Bank of England web si~~te~~
www.bankofengland.co.uk

May 2002

Northwick Park Road, Harrow, Middlesex

Our National Hero Sven-Goran Eriksson
The Football Association
Soho Square
London
W1

26th June 2002

Dear Sven

You are a hero!

So much so that I have written to the Bank of England to ask them if they will feature you as the first foreigner on the new £50 note. I think they will need some suitable source material.

Please can you send me a signed photograph? I think that what you have achieved is fantastic and I would really value adding your autograph to my collection.

Kind regards

John Summers

A man of few words ...
well just one word
actually ...

Sven-Göran Eriksson
Head Coach

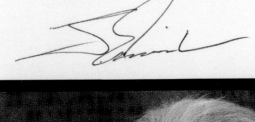

Northwick Park Road, Harrow, Middlese

Joe Lovejoy hears Sven-Göran Eriksson deliver a strong vote of confidence for his grief-stricken keeper

SVEN-GÖRAN ERIKSSON is prepared to keep faith with David Seaman, despite the mistake that ended England's World Cup hopes on Friday. Before leaving Japan for home yesterday, Eriksson said Seaman would continue to be his first-choice goalkeeper next season at the age of 39, with the proviso that he was playing regularly for Arsenal.

Far from terminating the keeper's intern...
the...

John Witherow
The Editor
The Sunday Times
1 Pennington Street
London
E98 1ST

24th June 2002

Dear Mr Witherow

I am a little bit confused by what was written in your fine paper yesterday.

On page 24 of the News section, Maurice Chittenden and Robert Winnett wrote a joint article (who holds the pen then!?) Referring to Sven-Goran Ericksson, they reported:

> *Asked if he would again pick David Seaman, the goalkeeper beaten by Ronaldinho's winning free kick in Friday's quarter-final, he said: "I have no idea about that. I think it is a problem that will solve itself."*

Yet by the time that we, your loyal readerbase, had arrived at page 7 of the Sport section, Joe Lovejoy had written:

> *Before leaving Japan for home yesterday, Ericksson said Seaman would continue to be his first-choice goalkeeper next season at the age of 39.*

What is going on here!? I have a few theories – which of these is true?

1. As Sven predicted, the problem solved itself between page 24 of the News section and page 7 of the Sport section.
2. Sven gave an interview to one journalist while an imposter spoke to the other. (I know that I have had trouble with imposters in the past.)
3. Maurice Chittenden and Robert Winnett's joint article suffered from the substantial effort required to hold the one pen between them.

I enclose £5 that I would like you to put towards the *John Summers Chair for Journalistic Studies* at a university of your choice. Please let me know which.

Kind regards

John Summers

THE SUNDAY TIMES

1 Pennington Street, London E98 1ST *Telephone: 020 7782 5640 Fax: 020 7782 5420*

From the Editor

Mr J Summers
█ Northwick Park Road
Harrow
Middlesex HA1 2NY

July 4, 2002

Dear Mr Summers,

Thank you for your amusing letter, and the fiver, which I am returning so you can fund your own chair.

I gather this quote came from the same interview and I'm not sure they are mutually exclusive. The first point he mentions is not carried in its entirety – it should go on to say that if Seaman plays for Arsenal he would be Eriksson's first choice.

The second is a summary of what Eriksson said, and therefore more complete. I accept that the first could be misleading in that you, our loyal readerbase, could conclude that he meant to drop Seaman.

All in all, it looks as if the news journalists were trying to raise a question mark when none exists. But who knows? Maybe they'll be proved prescient.

Yours sincerely

John Witherow

Registered Office: Times Newspapers Limited, 1 Virginia Street, London E98 1XY
Registered No. 894646 England & Wales

The Old Rectory,

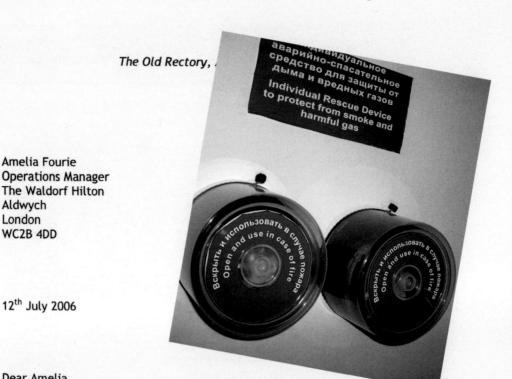

аварийно-спасательное
средство для защиты от
дыма и вредных газов
Individual Rescue Device
to protect from smoke and
harmful gas

Вскрыть и использовать в случае пожара
Open and use in case of fire

Amelia Fourie
Operations Manager
The Waldorf Hilton
Aldwych
London
WC2B 4DD

12th July 2006

Dear Amelia

I've just come back from Moscow. What a fine city it is! In parts.

I stayed in a wonderful hotel, a sturdy hotel that has been around for over 100 years. One particular aspect really intrigued me. To protect me in the unlikely event of a fire, my room came equipped with a smoke-hood (a bit like a Storm-Trooper's respirator). I've also stayed in your hotel yet there was no smoke-hood in my room.

As we all know, smoke is one of the biggest killers when it comes to fires. So, if we don't have these hoods in Britain, does it mean that we think our lives are worth less than those of the Russians?

Please let me know if it is still safe to sleep in your magnificent, but strangely smoke-hood-free, rooms.

Kind regards

John Summers

The Waldorf Hilton

17th July 2006

Mr John Summers
The Old Ractory

Devon

Dear Mr Summers

Re: The Waldorf Hilton

Thank you for taking the time to write to us following your stay in Moscow.

Here at The Waldorf Hilton we pride ourselves in our fire safety procedures and precautions. I can confirm that we have smoke detection equipment installed in every single room and all public areas. We also patrol the entire building and perimeter 4 times daily to spot any possible fire hazards. Over and above this we test our fire alarm weekly to measure the audibility of its alarm bells.

I can confirm that our rooms are certainly very safe to stay in and that we have each guest who stays with us best interest at heart, especially when it comes to fire safety.

Once again thank you for your letter and we look forward to welcoming you back to The Waldorf Hilton in hopefully the not too distant future.

With renewed apologies and kindest regards

Yours sincerely
THE WALDORF HILTON

Anelia Fourie
Security Manager

The Waldorf Hilton
Aldwych, London WC2B 4DD England
Tel: +44 (0)20 7836 2400 Fax: +44 (0)20 7836 7244
VAT Registration Number GB 240 1132 31

hilton.co.uk/waldorf

Adda Hotels Unlimited, Registered in England No. 879456
Registered Office: Maple Court, Central Park, Reeds Crescent, Watford,
Herts WD24 4QQ England

The Old Rectory, Devon

The Director in charge of New Policy
Corporate Headquarters
Marriott International
Marriott Drive
Washington DC
USA 20058

1st August 2006

Dear Sir or Madam

I've just come back from Moscow. What a fine city it is! In parts.

I stayed in a wonderful hotel, a sturdy hotel that has been around for over 100 years. One particular aspect really intrigued me. My room came equipped with a smoke-hood (a bit like a Storm-Trooper's respirator). I didn't try it on but presumably I could smoke inside it.

I've also stayed in some of your hotels in the USA yet have never found a smoke-hood in my room.

Last week I received an electronic mail (e-mail) from you telling me all about your new smoke-free policy in North America. Would it not have been easier to install Russian-style smoke-hoods in the rooms for those who want to smoke? That way, you could please all your guests all of the time?

Will you take up this advice when you extend your policy to the UK?

Kind regards

John Summers

Marriott International, Inc.
Corporate Headquarters

Marriott Drive
Washington, D.C. 20058
301/380-3000

August 18, 2006

Mr. John Summers
The Old Rectory

Devon,
United Kingdom

Dear Mr. Summers:

Thank you for your letter regarding Marriott's new "smoke-free" policy for all North American properties.

This decision reflects the preference of the vast majority of our guests, including our Marriott Rewards members, for a smoke-free experience. While this room type is no longer offered, we do offer special designated smoking areas outside for our guests.

We appreciate your comments regarding the possibility of using smoke-hoods as an option for those guests who wish to smoke in the hotel guest rooms. While the decision has been made to go entirely "smoke-free" in the North American properties it may still be an option in our International properties. We will keep your suggestion in mind as we review our International hotel smoking standards.

Thank you for your feedback. We appreciate your business and look forward to welcoming you again soon.

Sincerely,

Michelle Longson
Regional Liaison
Mr. Marriott's Office

Northwick Park Road, Harrow, Middlesex

Hugh Sumner
Head of Infraco Sub-Surface Lines
Transport*for*London
Windsor House
42-50 Victoria Street
London
SW1H 0TL

2nd May 2002

Dear Mr Sumner,

I wrote to you over 7 years ago about a fundamental design flaw in your trains and I see that this has still not been resolved. On the Circle Line you have used solid metal handrails hanging from the ceiling rather than those old flexible springy ones.

I am 6'6" tall yet your bars only leave room for a dwarf of 6' to pass underneath. This contravenes building regulations. The position of the bars is extremely dangerous and I am sick of bashing my head on them. The problem is made worse by the fact that your trains are so crowded that people often push me into your rigid bars. This is very painful.

In Nov 1994 I received a reply from London Underground which told me about your new trains but made no reference to solving this problem. One comment indicated that trains would become less crowded but, 7 years later, that problem still exists.

Do you intend to make your trains safe in the next 7 years? If so, then when please?

Kind regards

John Summers

⊖ UNDERGROUND

Infraco Sub-Surface Limited

30 The South Colonnade
Canary Wharf
London E14 5EU

Mr John Summers
▓▓ Northwick Park Road
Harrow
Middlesex
HA1 2NY

Dear Mr Summers

Thank you for your letter dated 2nd May 2002. It is always appreciated to receive positive as well as negative feedback from customers.

You will know doubt have seen in the national press and on television, that London Underground and their new private sector partners Metronet and Tubelines, are about to embark on a massive investment programme over the next 30 years under the PPP Agreement to enhance the underground's assets.

During 2002/2003 (ISSL) Infraco Sub-Surface Limited are gearing up for a major enhancement programme, which will include: modification and refurbishment packages to improve the safety and reliability even further to our three fleets of trains which includes the Circle Line.

Over the next 10 years, 40 new six or seven car trains on the Hammersmith and Circle Lines will be introduced, with restyled cars with the latest designs eliminating all the problems you have mentioned in your letter and experienced in the past. The trains will be walkthrough with CCTV security and text information to customers.

Thank you again for taking the trouble to write: you will see improvements to ISSL's assets, especially our fleet of trains now this massive investment programme is underway.

Yours sincerely

[signature: Hugh Sumner]

Hugh Sumner
Managing Director, Infraco Sub-Surface Limited

Copy to:

Customs Declaration Form (left)

WELCOME TO THE UNITED STATES

DEPARTMENT OF THE TREASU
UNITED STATES CUSTOMS SER'

CUSTOMS DECLARATIO

19 CFR 122.27, 148.12, 148.13, 148.110, 148.11

arriving traveler or responsible family mem
g information (only **ONE** written declaration pe

y name

(Given) Name   3. Middle Initia

e/Flight No. or Vessel Name or Vehicle License No.

Country of Citizenship   7. (b) Count

U.S. Address (Street Number/Hotel/Mailing Address

U.S. Address (City)   8. (c) U.S.

ountries visited on this trip prior to U.S. arrival
    b.
    d.

The purpose of my (our) trip is or was:
(Check one or both boxes, if applicable)

1. I am (We are) bringing fruits, plants, meats, food, soil, birds, snails, other live animals, wildlife products, farm products; or, have been on a farm or ranch outside the U.S.:

2. I am (We are) carrying currency or monetary instruments over $10,000 U.S., or foreign equivalent

3. I have (We have) commercial merchandise, U.S. or foreign: (Check one box only)

14. The total value of all goods, including commercial merchandise, I/we purchased or acquired abroad and am/are bringing to the U.S. is:

(See the instructions on the back of this form unde provided there to list all the items you must declare. in the space provided above).

SIGN BELOW AFTER YOU REA

I have read the notice on the reverse and

X

Letter (center)

Northwick Park Road, Harrow, Middlesex

Ambassador William S Farish
The American Embassy
24 Grosvenor Square
London
W1A 1AE

2nd May 2002

Dear Ambassador,

I have a simple question that has me intrigued. Recently I went on my first trip to America and I was surprised by your temporary immigration form. It asked me to declare such things as whether I was a terrorist, a paedophile or a Nazi!

Have you ever succeeded in catching people out this way? If so then the printing of these questions must have saved hours of intensive police work. Please can you tell me how many people you have arrested as a result of self-confessed declarations on your forms?

I look forward to receiving a response from you.

Kind regards

John Summers

Form (bottom left)

Do any of the following app

A. Do you have a communicab disorder; or are you a drug abu

B. Have you ever been arrested or c involving moral turpitude or c substance; or been arrested or con for which the aggregate sentence or more; or been a controlled sub seeking entry to engage in criminal or immoral activities?

C. Have you ever been or are you now involved in espionage o sabotage; or in terrorist activities; or genocide; or between 1933 and 1945 were you involved, in any way, in persecutions associated with Nazi Germany or its allies?

D. Are you seeking to work in the U.S.; or have you ever been excluded and deported; or been previously removed from th United States; or procured or attempted to pre entry into the U.S. by fraud or misr

Form (bottom right)

OMB No. 11115-01

U.S. Department of Justice
Immigration and Naturalization Service

Welcome to the United States

I-94W Nonimmigrant Visa Waiver Arrival/Departure Form

Instructions

This form must be completed by every nonimmigrant visitor not in poss of a visitor's visa, who is a national of one of the countries enumerated i 217. The airline can provide you with the current list of eligible countr

Type or print legibly with pen in ALL CAPITAL LETTERS. USE EN

This form is in two parts. Please complete both the Arrival Record, 11 and the Departure Record, items 14 through 17. The rever

U.S. Department of Justice

Immigration and Naturalization Service

Embassy of the United States of America
5 Upper Grosvenor Street
London W1A 2JB

July 5, 2002

John Summers
Northwick Park Road
Harrow
Middlesex
HA1 2NY

Dear Mr. Summers:

Your letters of 2 May 2002 and 12 June 2002 to Ambassador Farish concerning questions found on official forms used by the U.S. Immigration & Naturalization Service have been referred to this office for response.

The questions you refer to which are found on Form I-94W are valuable not only to the immigration inspection process for the current and future applications for admission to the United States, but also are valuable in the removal of undesirable persons from the United States.

I hope that this information will be of assistance to you.

Sincerely,

Edward H. Skerrett
Officer in Charge

Northwick Park Road, Harrow, Middlesex

Michael Burke
BBC Television Centre
White City
London
W12

10th July 2002

Dear Michael

I think it's great that you've gone head-to-head with your main news broadcast at the same time as ITN.

I never used to watch their news programme, not even if I missed yours. Now I definitely can't watch theirs. I tried it once. I wonder why Trevor McDonald is the Queen's favourite? And she gave him a knighthood as well!

So, when will Michael become Sir Michael? That's what our household wants to know. And would they let you read out your own newsstory?

So how can I help? I'd like to nominate you but I'm not sure what the official process is. Do I just write to the Queen and then that's it sorted?

Finally, please can you send me a smiley photo of yourself for my collection?

Kind regards

John Summers

News

Ten O'Clock News

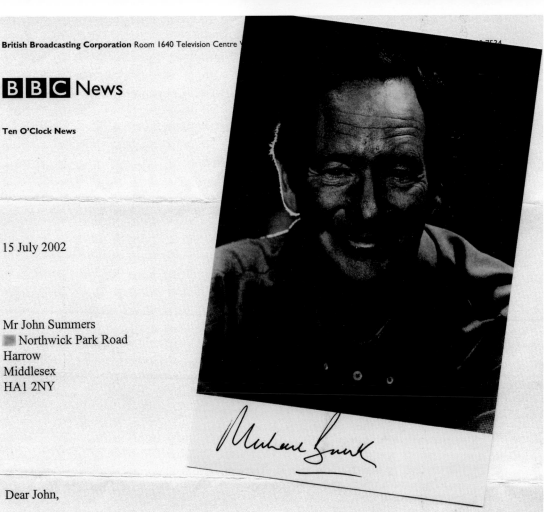

15 July 2002

Mr John Summers
Northwick Park Road
Harrow
Middlesex
HA1 2NY

Dear John,

Thanks for the kind thoughts. Please don't write to the Queen - or anybody else. Your powers of persuasion may be unlimited, but I am sure they could be deployed in a more worthwhile cause than stroking the overdeveloped egos of superannuated newscasters.

Have a (carefully airbrushed) photo instead.

Best wishes,

MICHAEL BUERK

Northwick Park Road, Harrow, Middlesex

Sir Trevor McDonald
ITN News At Ten
200 Grays Inn Road
London
WC1X 8XZ

10th July 2002

Dear Sir Trevor

I think it's great that you've gone head-to-head with your main news broadcast at the same time as the BBC.

I never used to watch their news programme, not even if I missed yours. Now I definitely can't watch theirs. I tried it once. No wonder the Queen gave you the knighthood!

Did you get some land and a coat-of-arms off Her Majesty when you were knighted? If not, I might be able to help. Not with the land – we only have a small garden and the kids really need it for football. But I could assist on the coat-of-arms front.

So how can I help? Tell me a bit about your great great great great great grandfather and then I'll send you some designs. Free! No catch! No 'see now pay later' scam.

Whether you wish to take up this offer or not, please can you send me a smiley photo of yourself for my collection?

Kind regards

John Summers

200 Gray's Inn Road
London WC1X 8XZ
Telephone (020) 7833 3000

John Summers
███ Northwick Park Road
Harrow
Middlesex
HA1 2NY

15th July, 2002

Dear Mr Summers,

Thank you so much for writing to Sir Trevor. He is delighted that you enjoy his programmes and sincerely hopes that we can count on you to keep watching

Thank you very much for taking the time and the trouble to write and I hope you like the photograph.

Yours sincerely,

Samantha Braund
PA to Sir Trevor McDonald, OBE

Registered Office 200 Gray's Inn Road London WC1X 8XZ Registered Number 548648
Independent Television News Limited

Northwick Park Road, Harrow, Middlesex

Sir Trevor McDonald
ITN News At Ten
200 Grays Inn Road
London
WC1X 8XZ

27th September 2002

Dear Sir Trevor

I short while ago I wrote to you on the subject of your well-deserved knighthood. As requested, you sent me a beaming photograph. Thank you - it's good to have your face brightening up our kitchen wall (and it covers up an old stain)!

Unfortunately you did not answer the second part of my letter. Basically I would like to know if you received some land and a coat-of-arms off Her Majesty when you were knighted? If not, I can assist on the coat-of-arms front.

Please can you tell me a little bit about your great great great great great grandfather, or anything relevant about your family's roots, and then I'll send you some designs. Free! No catch! No 'see now pay later' scam.

I look forward to hearing back from you.

Kind regards

John Summers

200 Gray's Inn Road
London WC1X 8XZ
Telephone (020) 7833 3000

John Summers
▓ Northwick Park Road
Harrow
Middlesex
HA1 2NY

7th October, 2002

Dear John Summers,

Thank you for your letter of 27th September. You might not believe this but the day on which I received my knighthood is all a bit of a blur. That probably is something to do with the fact that after the Palace I repaired to a nearby hostelry for a very long, enjoyable and very boozy lunch.

I am pretty sure a coat of arms never came into the reckoning but I would hate to bet the mortgage on it! I am delighted that you received the picture.

Yours sincerely,

Sir Trevor McDonald, OBE

Registered Office 200 Gray's Inn Road London WC1X 8XZ Registered Number 548648 England
Independent Television News Limited

Northwick Park Road, Harrow, Middlesex

Professor Timothy J Pedley, FRS
Head of Department of Applied Mathematics & Theoretical Physics
University of Cambridge
Silver Street
Cambridge
CB3 9EW

10th July 2002

Dear Professor Pedley

I've managed to tie myself up in knots with a mathematical conundrum. As the country's top mathematics expert, please can you untie me?

Here's the problem. To make it easy to explain, let's take two characters, say Posh and Becks. Posh starts 1 km ahead of Becks and runs off at 0.1 metre / second. Becks sets off ten times faster to chase her at 1 metre / second (he is, after all, the England captain).

Now this is the difficult bit. In the time it takes Becks to run the 1km, Posh will have moved forwards an additional 100 metres. So he runs forwards another 100 metres only to find that the object of his desire is now 10 metres in front. And when, in a rather frustrated manner, he covers that 10 metres, Posh will have put another metre between them. Etc.

Clearly the distance between them will get smaller, but it seems that Becks will never actually catch Posh. Yet he is running ten times faster!

Mathematically speaking, what is going on here? It's driving me mad!

Kind regards

John Summers

UNIVERSITY OF CAMBRIDGE
Department of Applied Mathematics and Theoretical Physics
Silver Street, Cambridge, England CB3 9EW

From: Professor T.J. Pedley FRS
G.I. Taylor Professor of Fluid Mechanics
Head of Department
Tel: ██████████
Fax: ██████████
E-mail: ██████████

12 July, 2002

Mr John Summers
██ Northwick Park Road
Harrow
Middlesex HA1 2NY

Dear Mr Summers

Thank you for your note. I don't think most of my colleagues would agree with the designation "the country's top mathematics expert", but your conundrum is a familiar one. Indeed, it was known to the Ancient Greeks and these days is called "Zeno's paradox". *

The fallacy in your argument is to suppose that each step in the process (100 metres, 10 metres, 1 metre, …) takes the same amount of time. If that were the case it would indeed take an infinite amount of time for B to overtake P (though, as in an old joke concerning the difference between applied and pure mathematicians, it would only take a finite time to get close enough for all practical purposes). In fact, however, the time for each step would decrease in the same proportion (1000 seconds, 100 seconds, 10 seconds, …). Thus the distance run by P $(100 + 10 + 1 + \ldots =$ ~~xxxxxx~~ 111.11…metres) would take ten times that many seconds. Precisely at that time B would have run ten times as far and would have just caught up with P. After 112 seconds, say, B would be ahead.

I hope this helps.

Yours sincerely

Tim Pedley

Professor T J Pedley

* a "Achilles & the tortoise"

UNIVERSITY OF OXFORD

Mathematical Institute

Chairman of Mathematics
Dr N.M.J. Woodhouse

24-29 St Giles', Oxford OX1 3LB
Enquiries: +44 (0) 1865 273525
Direct line: +44 (0) 1865 ████
Secretary: +44 (0) 1865 ████
Fax: +44 (0) 1865 ████
████@maths.ox.ac.uk
http://www.maths.ox.ac.uk

25 July 2002

Mr John Summers
██ Northwick Park Road
Harrow
Middlesex
HA1 2NY

Dear Mr Summers

This is an ancient paradox. In fact Becks catches up with Posh after T seconds, where

$$1000 + T/10 = T.$$

You can solve this to get

$$T = 10000/9 = 1111.11 \ldots \text{ seconds.}$$

The paradox arises because you are dividing this interval of T seconds into an infinite sum of smaller and smaller intervals:

$$T = 1000 + 100 + 10 + 1 + 0.1 + 0.01 + \ldots$$

just as the infinite decimal expansion of T suggests. However many of these smaller and smaller intervals you include, you never look at what happens beyond T seconds from the start. You therefore never look at what happens after Becks overtakes Posh.

I don't think you are fair to Posh. I am sure that she can run a lot faster than that!

Best wishes

Nick Woodhouse

Nick Woodhouse
Chairman of Mathematics

Northwick Park Road, Harrow, Middlesex

Allan Leighton
Chairman
Consignia plc
148 Old Street
London
EC1V 9HQ

20th June 2002

Dear Mr Leighton

I am surprised that you are changing your name from Consignia to the Royal Mail Group plc. Why on earth have you chosen that particular name? For a start it will remind people of an organisation that used to exist in this country not so long ago. They were called The Royal Mail.

Secondly, how can you justify the word "Royal"? There may well have been one million people on the Mall for the Queen's Golden Jubilee, but that leaves another 58,755,700 who weren't.

Also I believe that the name is a little too sexist when pronounced on the radio. Remember that we all live in contemporary times now!

So, my suggestion is that you call yourself the People's Post plc. This will enable you to communicate clearly what it is that you do as well as avoid upsetting anyone.

When can I expect to see the People's Post plc logo on our local van?

Kind regards

Jane Summers

Jane Summers

From the Chairman's office

24 June 2002

Jane Summers
███ Northwick Park Road
HARROW
HA1 2NY

Dear Ms Summers

Thank you for your letter of 20 June to Allan Leighton. I have been asked to reply.

Royal Mail is a well-known and trusted brand name, which has been around for some time and represents our letters and packets service. When we decided that we would change the name back from Consignia plc, we felt it was appropriate to opt for a name that had clearer connections with our brand names.

I am sorry that you dislike the name and note your reasoning for this. However, we will not be opting for "People's Post plc" as you have suggested, but thank you for your thoughts.

Kind regards

Yours sincerely

Gerry Durbin
Assistant to the Chairman

Group Centre, 5th Floor, 148 Old Street, LONDON, EC1V 9HQ
Tel: 020 7250 2888 Fax: 020 7250 2174
e-mail: gerry.durbin@consignia.com

The Old Rectory, Devon

Customer Services Team
McVitie's
Ashby-de-la-Zouch
Leicestershire
LE65 1NZ

25th May 2006

Dear Sir or Madam

Tasty! That's the word that I'd use for your NEW Chocolate Fruit & Nut
Caramel Shortcake Moments.

The only thing is that there aren't many of them inside the pack. Let me
explain. I've taken the 6 biscuits out, crushed them up and put them in my
measuring jug. (Actually I couldn't really crush the raisins but I sort of gooed
them into the bottom of the jug.) All 6 biscuits took up 153 cl which, I'm sure
that my Physics teacher Mr Bignull used to tell me, is 153 cm^3.

The box itself measures 4 x 24 x 9.5 cm = 912 cm^3. This means you actually
have space for 35 biscuits. You can imagine how happy that would make me!
So, please can you reshape your biscuits so that you can fit more in? You can
either go for cubes or rectangles – I don't mind which.

Kind regards

John Summers

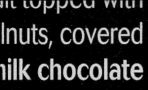

United Biscuits

McVitie's
Consumer Services Department
PO Box 7249
Ashby-de-la-Zouch
Leicestershire
LE65 2ZH

Telephone: 0500 011710
Facsimile: 01530 411888

Mr John Summers
The Old Rectory

Devon

Our Ref: 2006/23/026035 SG   05 June 2006

Dear Mr Summers

Thank you for contacting us about McVities Moments Chocolate Fruit & Nut Caramel Shortcake. We are sorry to hear that you were disappointed with your purchase. On behalf of McVitie's please accept my apologies for any inconvenience you may have experienced.

The packaging of our products is under constant review and great care, attention and research is given to the development of new packaging. Our first concern is to ensure that the product is effectively protected against damage or contamination in transit. We also aim to package our products in ways which reflect how people prefer to use them.

We take our responsibilities for the environment very seriously and try to balance all aspects of protection, presentation, promotion and cost as carefully as we can. We appreciate the concerns of our consumers and your comments will be passed on to our Marketing department.

We certainly never aim to wrap our products in more packaging than is necessary to give them maximum protection as this would add to the cost for both ourselves and the consumer.

Your help in bringing this to our attention is very much appreciated and as a gesture of goodwill please accept the enclosed reimbursement which can be used to purchase McVitie's products at your local store or all major supermarkets.

Yours sincerely

Sue Gibson
Consumer Services Co-Ordinator

United Biscuits (UK) Limited
Registered in England number 2506007
Registered Office: Hayes Park, Hayes End Road, Hayes, Middlesex UB4 8EE

Her Majesty The Queen
Buckingham Palace
The Mall
London

5th January 1991

Your Majesty

I have a question for you as I am a bit confused by this democracy thing. If I write a letter to you (as I am doing now) then how can I know whether you will see it or not?

If you don't see it then who chooses whether you see it or not? Surely that's the person who's really ruling the country? How can this be democratic when this letter is addressed to you, not your 'doorkeeper'?

So, how many letters do you read each week and have you seen this letter yourself?

Kind regards

John Summe

Her Majesty The Queen
Buckingham Palace
The Mall
London

2nd May 2002

Your Majesty,

Congratulations on 50 years on the throne!

I have a question for you as I am a bit confused by this democracy thing. If I write a letter to you (as I am doing now) then how can I know whether you will see it or not?

If you don't see it then who chooses whether you see it or not? Surely that's the person who's really ruling the country? How can this be democratic when this letter is addressed to you, not your 'doorkeeper'?

So, how many letters do you read each week and have you seen this letter yourself?

Kind regards

John Summers

BUCKINGHAM PALACE

22nd January, 1991.

Aha! 10 years on and the formality is falling...

Dear Mr Summers,

I am commanded by The Queen to write and thank you for your letter, which Her Majesty opened personally.

You may like to know that approximately two hundred letters are received each day, and although, as I am sure you will appreciate, it is not possible for The Queen to reply to them personally, all of Her Majesty's mail is sent to her each day before being dealt with by a member of The Queen's Household.

I enclose a leaflet which you may like to have and I am to thank you for your interest.

Yours sincerely,

Mawba.

BUCKINGHAM PALACE

4th July, 2002

Dear Mr Summers,

The Queen has asked me to thank you for your letter of 2nd May and I apologise for the delay in replying. As I am sure you will appreciate, Her Majesty has received an exceptionally large number of letters in recent months as a result of the anniversary of her Accession and the deaths of Queen Elizabeth and Princess Margaret.

I can confirm that The Queen does see all the letters she receives but as I am sure you will understand, it is not possible currently for her to do this, bearing in mind the very large quantity that Buckingham Palace are receiving.

I hope this will help to answer your query and thank you for taking the time and trouble to write as you did.

Yours sincerely,

Northwick Park Road, Harrow, Middlesex

Gordon Adie
MD
Konecranes (UK) Ltd
2 Peel Park Place
College Milton
East Kilbride
G74 5LR

23rd September 2002

Dear Gordon

Please can you help me provide a service to other captains of industry? In these contemporary times we need to compress huge amounts of information into a tiny soundbite.

I can think of no-one better than you to demonstrate this.

As MD of Konecranes, a leading manufacturer of elevating machinery, please can you tell me what your elevator speech is?

Kind regards

John Summers

 **KONECRANES**

4th November 2002

Mr John Summers.
▮ Northwick Park Road,
Middlesex.
HA1 2NY.

Dear Sir,

Thank you for your letter of 23rd September 2002 and your description of an "Elevator speech".

The lateness of my response is nothing to do with this being a difficult exercise, I have been travelling extensively and it is only now that I am catching up on the non-essential items in my mail.

I am intrigued a little by the request, and as to why you want this description from me, and for what purpose, however the following best describes what I believe I do.

"I am responsible for the day to day operation of KONECRANES (UK) Ltd, a subsidiary of KCI KONECRANES International Plc. My duties are to manage people to get the best performance from them to the benefit of the company, putting skills correctly where they are best utilised. I also ensure that we cover all aspects of risk in the contracts we accept, including the performance of these contracts and that we are able to provide a product that benefits our clients business while being profitable in our business".

Very brief, but descriptive in general terms. I have a multi-role in our organisation and hopefully this gives a flavour, or else the story runs for pages.

Yours Sincerely,

Gordon W Adie
Managing Director

KONECRANES (UK) Ltd.   **KCI KONECRANES GROUP**

☐ Peel Park Place, College Milton   ☐ Registered in Scotland   ☐ Ultimate Holding Co:
   East Kilbride, Glasgow, G74 5LR   No. 75148   KCI Konecranes International
   Tel +44-(0)13552-20591
   Fax +44-(0)13552-63654

Northwick Park Road, Harrow, Middlesex

Nicholas Serota
Director and Chairman of the Jury
Tate Britain
Millbank
London
SW1P 4RG

9th July 2002

Dear Mr Serota

Do you see what I've done here? I've created a reaction. An interaction. A meeting of minds, at least in understanding. Possibly even in conviction.

And in so doing, I have created the seeds of a relationship. But herein lies the difference. While the original intention was the creation of a private communication entre nous, now is the time to share this with the world.

The paint-brush is dead. The canvas is for history lessons. The written word is the new art. The PC is its servant.

Previous *Turner Prize* entrants have had to display several exhibits. Away with this precedent! Rules are just there for those who need to be bound by them.

Take this letter. Frame it. Position it. Light it. Display it. And let it be judged.

I await the jury's verdict with anticipation.

Kind regards

John Summers

John Summers

Millbank
London SW1P 4RG

call
+44 (0) 20 7887 8000
fax
+44 (0) 20 7887 8007

visit
www.tate.org.uk

TATE

TG4.2
TP2002

29 July 2002

John Summers Esq
Northwick Park Road
Harrow
Middlesex
HA1 2NY

Dear Mr Summers

Thank you for your letter of 9 July. I was interested to learn about your work, but as you will be aware, the jury has decided not to include your name on the shortlist for the Turner Prize this year.

Yours sincerely,

Sir Nicholas Serota
Director

Northwick Park Road, Harrow, Middlesex

Mark Rylance
Artistic Director
Shakespeare's Globe
21 New Globe Walk
London
SE1 9DT

8th July 2002

Dear Mark

What a wonderful theatre!

Recently I went to see *A Midsummer Night's Dream* by William Shakespeare. It reminded me of my school performance (I don't mean that yours was a childish approach! No, I was merely reminiscing about those halcyon days of youth.)

I think that the setting and atmosphere that you have created are totally unique. It's that special combination of building, actors and crowd which really struck me. I know that we all live in contemporary times but your wonderful creation really took me back to what it might have been like in the bard's time.

Except one thing.

Those wretched jumbo jets that screamed across the sky at regular intervals. To misquote, it seems that "There are more things in heaven and earth, Horatio, than were dreamt of in Shakespeare's philosophy". I think that it is totally insensitive of the air traffic controllers to route their craft directly over your theatre. Have you written to them to complain? Perhaps it hasn't occurred to them that they are ruining a piece of living history? I ask you, what is more important: flying over a bunch of champagned-up business executives for a meeting that could have been conducted by telephone or presenting art in its purest possible form?

Please tell me what you will be able to do to get rid of this airborne menace.

Kind regards

John Summers

Northwick Park Road
Harrow
Middlesex
HA1 2NY

Dear Mr Summers,

Thank you for you comments about the Globe and I was particularly pleased to hear how much you enjoyed *A Midsummer Night's Dream*. It is great to hear that what we are trying to achieve at the Globe has such support from our customers.

In answer to your comments about the noise from planes flying over the Globe, we are in constant dialogue with Air Traffic Control, and they are where possible very receptive to the problems we experience as an open-air venue. Therein lies the problem, we are an open-air building in the centre of one of the world's major cities.

Bearing in mind the growth of airline travel and the increase of services in and out of City Airport Air Traffic Control endeavor not to route planes or helicopters over the Globe.

Helicopters are our particular problem. As a legal requirement, all single engine helicopters must fly up the Thames so that in case of an emergency they can jettison into the Thames rather than over occupied buildings. The Globes location next to the Thames therefore puts us in a difficult position.

We have good contacts at Air Traffic Control and they will advise us as to who the aircrafts that are flying above us belong to and where possible ask them to move on. However, some air traffic such as police helicopters who are in the process of doing their job we have understandably little control over.

I hope this will go some way to answering your concerns.

Yours sincerely,

Ian Pettitt
House Manager

SECRETARY

7832 5426
end@nats.co.uk

Dear Mr Summers

17 July 2002

VICTORIA OVEREND
National Air Traffic Serv
Room T1415, One Kemb
Direct Tel: +44 (0)20 7
Switchboard: +44 (0)2

Mr J Summe
Northwic
Harrow
Middlesey
HA1 2NY

Thank you for your letter dated 8 July 02 that you sent to Richard Everitt, he has asked me to respond on his behalf.

Whilst I agree that the Globe Theatre's setting is fantastic and the atmosphere created there is totally unique, unfortunately, it is underneath the one of the final approaches into Heathrow Airport, the use of which is governed by the runway in operation, weather conditions and particular operational circumstances.

As I am sure you are aware the airspace in the South East of England is complex and the ability to re-route traffic away from the area of the Globe would be incredibly difficult.

I am sorry that this is not the answer you were seeking and hope that your next visit to the Globe will not be so disturbed.

Yours sincerely,

V.Overe

V OVEREND

Dea

T'

As I
ability to re

75

Northwick Park Road, Harrow, Middlesex

Ken Livingstone
The Mayor of London
City Hall
The Queen's Walk
London SE1 2AA

23rd September 2002

Dear Ken

Yesterday's International Car Free Day was a success but why did you combine it with International Public Toilet Free Day?

I went up to Tower Bridge, expecting bridges and roads to be closed for the day. But I did not expect public toilets to be closed as well. The huge facilities opposite the Tower of London entrance were firmly shut at 11:00 a.m. Fortunately McDonalds restaurant offered its relatively limited facilities with open arms. The queue of women up the stairs and on the street was testament to that. (Or did McDonalds pay you to keep the public toilets closed so that more people would have to visit them?)

In addition, there was a huge snaking queue outside your wonderful £43,000,000 City Hall. I know, I was in it. A huge sign marked "toilets" was placed nearby. But it was mere tantalisation. Despite the crowds of people, there were only three loos! Now don't get me wrong, three is better than nothing. But I think that the steady stream of people zipping up their trousers, as they left the bushes, shows that this was not enough.

Are you planning International Car Free Day again? If so, will you try and make it more comfortable for us, the general public? Surely you can scrape together a few tenners to keep London's bowels moving?

Kind regards

John Summers

Public Liaison Unit

City Hall
The Queen's Walk
London SE1 2AA
Switchboard: 020 7983 4000
Minicom: 020 7983 4458
Web: www.london.gov.uk

Mr J Summers
⬛ Northwick Park Road
Harrow
Middlesex
HA1 2NY

Our ref: MGLA260902-6813
Your ref:
Date: 31 October 2002

Dear Mr Summers

Thank you for your letter of 23 September 2002 addressed to the Mayor of London, this has been passed to me for a reply. I apologise for the delay in replying, which is due to a backlog of correspondence caused by technical problems with our computer system.

I am sorry to learn that the lack of public toilet facilities may have made your trip to London less enjoyable recently. However, the provision of such facilities is not something that the Mayor and GLA have responsibility for, as it is a matter under the jurisdiction of the local authorities.

In addition, the provision of such facilities at events such as car free day and open house, is the responsibility of the event organisers. The Mayor of London did not organise car free day, but just hosted it.

This said though, the Mayor is aware that such facilities are lacking in London and through his London Plan will work with the boroughs to encourage them to provide better facilities in the future.

I am sorry not to be able to offer a more positive reply on this occasion but thank you for taking the time to write to the Mayor of London.

Yours sincerely

Nicola Dunderdale
Public Liaison Officer

Direct telephone: 020 7983 4100 Fax: 020 7983 4057 Email: mayor@london.gov.uk

Northwick Park Road, Harrow, Middlesex

Janet Lenz
Customer Service Director
McDonald's Restaurants Limited
11-59 High Road
East Finchley
London
N2 8AW

23rd September 2002

Dear Janet

In the last 24 hours I have been delighted and disgusted by McDonalds.

First the delight. I went up to Tower Bridge for International Car Free Day. While Ken Livingstone had declared that he was to close bridges and roads for the day, he did not point out that he would also close public toilets as well. The huge facilities opposite the Tower of London entrance were firmly shut at 11:00 a.m. Fortunately your restaurant offered its relatively limited facilities with open arms. The queue of women up the stairs and on the street was testament to that. So, well done! (Or did you authorise the closing of the public toilets so that more people would have to come and visit you?)

But then the disgust. Trying to find your address just now, I went onto the internet and put in ronaldmacdonald.com. Up popped Tina, with not a lot on. I did not look any further - my wife would not approve. (My friend Paddy would like it though.) Perhaps I'm just too old for your target market but is this how you really want to promote yourself to young people these days? I feel that you have undone all the good work that you did yesterday.

Kind regards

John Summers

Our Ref:RKF/550551/200

26th September 2002

Mr John Summers
▮ Northwick Park Road
Harrow
Middx
HA1 2NY

Dear Mr Summers

I am in receipt of your letter dated 23rd September 2002, sent for the attention of Janet Lenz, Head of Customer Services and forwarded to me for response.

You mention whilst visiting Tower Bridge on International Car Free Day, you were delighted to find that the McDonald's situated at Tower Hill, allowed members of the public to freely use their toilet facilities.

We are always delighted when customers take the time and trouble to contact us with their positive observations about our restaurants. Your comments are greatly appreciated and will be passed onto the whole restaurant team at Tower Hill.

I note with concern, however, that whilst attempting to find our website, you inadvertently came across another site which contained unsavory images. Please accept my apologies. As you may be aware anyone can purchase a domain name and in this case I must stress that we have absolutely no connection with the site you refer to in your correspondence.

For your information you may be interested to know that our website can be found at www.mcdonalds.co.uk.

Finally, I am sorry that your delight turned into disappointment, but hope that your overall impression of McDonald's will remain a positive one.

Yours sincerely

pp V. Bedwell

Rhonda Floyd
Customer Services Manager

INVESTOR IN PEOPLE

McDonald's Restaurants Limited
11-59 High Road, East Finchley, London N2 8AW
Telephone **08705 244 622** Facsimile 020 8700 7060

Registered Office 11-59 High Road, East Finchley, London N2 8AW
Registered in England No. 1002769

Northwick Park Road, Harrow, Middlesex

John Redshaw
General Manager
Rank Hovis
Clarence Flour Mills
Great Union Street
Hull
HU9 1AD

28th August 2002

Dear Mr. Redshaw

I have just returned from spending a blissfully short time in Hull.

Please can you tell me what that rather strange smell is over the harbour area near to The Deep? I wouldn't be surprised if I had detected fish and fish by-products but that smell has nothing at all fishy about it. Well that's not quite right. It is 'fishy' but not as in 'halibut' or 'monkfish'.

I saw your large sign saying 'rank'. Does that mean that it is your smell? If so, why are you so proud of it?

I asked several people at The Deep but they were quite unaware of the smell. Perhaps it is some sort of industrial mind-altering drug that has fogged their noses. Well what on earth does this have to do with milling flour?

I hope that you can resolve this mystery.

Kind regards

John Summers

21st November 2002

Mr. J. Summers
▓ Northwick Park Road
Harrow
Middlesex
HA1 2NY

Dear Mr. Summers,

I must apologise to you for the delay in replying to your letters but I moved from my role at the Hull mill some time ago.

I am surprised that you believe that our flour mill generated a smell that was strong enough to permeate the atmosphere at The Deep. The mill has recently celebrated its 50th birthday and I have no knowledge of a similar comment – Rank or not!

The process of transforming wheat to flour is mechanical and is not known for generating a strong 'pong'. I know the team at Hull are carrying out a major environmental management project and they would be very concerned if your comments prove to be correct.

If you have enough thoughts as to the cause or source of the smell, please let Mick Topham at the mill know as he is leading the environmental project.

Yours sincerely,

John Redshaw

Rank Hovis Limited
The Lord Rank Centre Lincoln Road High Wycombe Bucks. HP12 3QS
Telephone (0870) 728 1111 Business Service Centre (0870) 729 4200
Facsimile (01494) 428428 Telex 83145

Registered Office: Chapel House Liston Road Marlow Bucks. SL7 1TJ Registered in England No. 62065

The Old Rectory, Devon

Philippa Marshall
Cone Ranger
Ben & Jerry's Homemade Ltd
10 Charter Place
High Street
Egham
Surrey
TW20 9EA

22nd May 2006

Dear Philippa

Mmmmmmm or hic? That's my question.

Your new 'Dublin Mudslide' recipe sounds wonderful but I'm concerned about
how much alcohol there is in the Irish Cream Liqueur. How many scoops am I
allowed to eat before I go driving? And is there a standard size for these
scoops? How big is the risk of 'overdoing it' on this ice-cream?

Kind regards

John Summers

BEN&JERRY'S

Hi John,
There is 0.21% alcohol in a 102gm
serving of Dublin Mudside.
Best regards
        Ben & Jerry's

1st Floor, Goswell House,
Goswell Hill, Windsor,
Berkshire SL4 1DS
(t): +44 (0)1753 834034
(f): +44 (0)1753 834035
(e): euphoria@benjerry.co.uk
(w): www.benjerry.co.uk

Northwick Park Road, Harrow, Middlesex

The Rt Hon Estelle Morris, MP
Secretary of State for Education and Skills
Sanctuary Buildings
Great Smith Street
London SW1P 3BT

23rd September 2002

Dear Ms Morris

At one time, Britain used to be the envy of the world for her ruthless devotion
to progress. But recently, she demonstrated that this is no longer the case.

I am referring, of course, to the fact that a new road sign has been put up
outside Mount Stewart school in Kenton, Middlesex. What does this sign say?
"Humps for 140 yards".

In school, children learn things the metric way. As does much of the third
world. But when they leave the school gates, they see a brand new sign that
would be more at home outside *ye olde tea shoppe*. What is a yard? Why have
you chosen to use this outdated unit of measurement rather than rods, chains
or furlongs?

As Secretary of State for Education, what message do you think that this gives
to our children? When Anthony Wedgewood-Benn set up the Metrication Board
in 1969, the Labour Government set a target for the completion of metrication
by 1976. Since then you've had another 26 years. OK, perhaps a bit less with
the other side in power at times.

So come on! Sort out this old issue. Metrication was first proposed to
government on 13th April 1790 by Sir John Riggs Miller in Britain and the Bishop
of Autum, Prince Talleyrand in France. Can't you spur this issue forwards, at
least for the sake of our children?

The Ordnance Survey is already there with maps measured in kilometres. Much
of our former empire has adopted metrication. Why don't we catch up at the
same time that we introduce Euros?

Please tell me by what date the government will meet its 1976 target.

Kind regards

John Summers

department for
education and skills
creating opportunity, releasing potential, achieving excellence

**Public
Enquiry
Unit**

P.O. Box 12
Runcorn
Cheshire
WA7 2GJ

tel: 0870 000 2288
fax: 01928 794248
minicom: 01928 794274
info@dfes.gsi.gov.uk

John Summers
███ Northwick Park Road
Harrow
Middlesex
HA1 2NY

PEU Reference No: 20946

Date: 26 September 2002

Dear Mr Summers,

Thank you for your letter of 23rd September 2002, addressed to the Secretary of State.

The issues you raise however, are a matter for the Department for Transport, Local Government and the Regions and I am transferring your correspondence to them for a reply to you direct. If you wish to contact them, they can be contacted at the address below:

> Department for Transport, Local Government and the Regions
> Postal Room
> Eland House
> Bressenden Place
> London
> SW1E 5DU
>
> Telephone Number: 0207 944 3333

Yours sincerely

Paula Southall
Department for Education and Skills

INVESTOR IN PEOPLE

John Summers
███ Northwick Park Road
Harrow
Middx
HA1 2NY

20 December 2002

Dear Mr Summers

Thank you for your recent communication.

I appreciate that you believe the NUT is able to influence the Government across the board, including road signs. The NUT concerns itself with education provision and the concerns of teachers. As you recognise metrication is taught in schools and children of today are fully conversant with this sytem. I have noted that you raise this issue with me because of the proximity of the road sign to a school. Unfortunately such a situation does not make the issue of road signs a legitimate concern for the Union.

Your concerns about road/street signs are rather for the Department for Transport and the Regions or perhaps for the motoring associations. You may also wish to take up the issue with the planning department of your local authority.

Yours sincerely

DOUG McAVOY
General Secretary

NATIONAL UNION OF TEACHERS HEADQUARTERS

HAMILTON HOUSE MABLEDON PLACE LONDON WC1H 9BD
TELEPHONE 020 7388 6191   FAX 020 7387 8458

GENERAL SECRETARY: DOUG McAVOY   DEPUTY GENERAL SECRETARY: STEVE SINNOTT

Northwick Park Road, Harrow, Middlesex

Chris Walker
Chief Planning Officer
The London Borough of Brent
Brent House
Wembley
Middlesex   HA9 3AD

4th February 2003

Dear Mr Walker

You would not believe the trouble I have had to obtain a simple answer to a simple question! But, at last, I have found the man responsible. I have asked the Education Secretary, the Department for Transport Traffic Management Division, the National Union of Teachers and Anthony Wedgewood-Benn. Their combined responses point a finger at you! You are the man who will make sense of all this. Congratulations.

So, please explain why a new road sign has been put up outside Mount Stewart school in Kenton with the message: "Humps for 140 yards"?

In school, children learn things the metric way. As does much of the third world. But when they leave the school gates, they see a brand new sign that would be more at home outside *ye olde tea shoppe*. What is a yard? Why have you chosen to use this particular outdated unit of measurement rather than hands, fathoms or furlongs?

Anthony Wedgewood-Benn set up the Metrication Board in 1969 and the Government set a target for the completion of metrication by the end 1975. That deadline was 27 years ago!

I know that I should expect politicians to carry on debating for another 27 years, but surely you can make a practical start here, in Brent, at least for the sake of our children? Please tell me what you can do to change this sign to "Humps for 128 metres".

Kind regards

John Summers

THE PLANNING SERVICE

CHRIS WALKER

DIRECTOR OF PLANNING

BRENT HOUSE,
349-357 HIGH ROAD,
WEMBLEY. HA9 6BZ
YOUR REF:
OUR REF: TPS/CCW/02/1982
CONTACT: Chris Walker
TELEPHONE: 020 8937 ▓▓▓
FACSIMILE: 020 8937 ▓▓▓
E-MAIL: ▓▓▓▓▓ @brent.gov.uk
WEB SITE:
http://www.brent.gov.uk/planning.nsf

Mr John Summers
▓▓ Northwick Park Road
Harrow
Middlesex
HA1 2NY

19 March 2003

Dear Mr. Summers

Town Country Planning Act 1990

<u>Signs outside Mount Stewart School</u>

Thank you for your letter of 4th February. I must apologise for the delay in my reply.

I fully understand the point that you make in your letter however having discussed the matter with colleagues in our Transportation Unit I am advised that the sign you refer to is required to make reference to yards by virtue of current legislation relating to road signage. Signs also currently are required to make reference to miles rather than kilometres.

Yours sincerely

Chris Walker
Director of Planning

The Old Rectory, Devon

Customer Service Centre
Ordnance Survey
Romsey Road
Southampton
SO16 4GU

22nd May 2006

Dear Sir or Madam

I am confused by your maps. They seem to be written for continental types rather than for us Brits. Let me explain.

I've seen a new road sign outside a school that says "Humps for 140 yards". And, all over the country, we can see signs that tell us things like "3½ miles to Nut Crackers". (Please don't laugh; it's a real village near here.)

So, why do you insist on printing maps with a kilometre grid? It seems that this can only help an invasion force more than it can possibly help us.

I know that Sir John Riggs Miller first proposed metrication to government on 13th April 1790. And Sir Anthony Wedgewood-Benn set up the Metrication Board in 1969. Also much of our former empire has adopted metrication. However, as today's government has decided to keep to the old-fashioned quaintness of miles, yards, rods, chains and furlongs why have you confused the issue by using kilometres?

Kind regards

John Summers

Ordnance Survey
Romsey Road
SOUTHAMPTON
United Kingdom
SO16 4GU

Business enquiries: +44 (0) 23 8030 5030
General enquiries (calls charged at local rate):
08456 05 05 05
Textphone (deaf and hard of hearing users only please):
+44 (0) 23 8079 2906
Email: customerservices@ordnancesurvey.co.uk
Website: www.ordnancesurvey.co.uk

Direct phone: 08456 05 05 05
Mobile:
Direct fax: 023 8079 2615
Email: customerservices@ordnancesurvey.co.uk

Our ref: SAP 56891
Your ref:

8 June 2006

Mr J Summers
The Old Rectory

Dear Mr Summers

RE: Ordnance Survey Mapping

Thank you for your letter dated 22 May 2006.

I have forwarded your correspondence to our technical department and they have confirmed the following:

The use of a metric grid on Ordnance Survey maps dates back to World War II. A Departmental Committee was set up under the chairmanship of Sir J.C.C. Davidson in 1935 to consider how the effectiveness of Ordnance Survey could be restored after the stringent government economies post-World War I had left Ordnance Survey ill-equipped to cope when new legislation such as the Town Planning Act, Land Registration Act, Housing Act and Land Valuation Act was introduced between 1925-31. The Final Report of the Davidson Committee was published in 1938. Two of its recommendations were that a National Grid be superimposed on all maps to provide a single reference system and that the international metre should be adopted as the unit on which the grid should be based.

The outbreak of World War II effectively meant these recommendations could not be put in to practice until after 1945 but the metric grid was introduced as soon as possible on all maps since then.

Government initiatives regarding metrication programmes in the 1960/70s meant that Ordnance Survey followed this lead; we introduced a programme of metric heighting/contours and we have converted our mapping to rational scales suitable for use with metric units, which also conform to recommendations by the International Standards Organisation. In today's computer age metric

units of measurement have become a necessary part of the use of all types of data including mapping.

As we are all aware the process of metrication has not been fully implemented in the UK and official use of miles and yards for distances is still in place. The conversion scales shown on our paper mapping have always been included to allow for either metric or imperial use for distance and height. However one thing we cannot do is lose the use of the metric grid.

I trust that you will find this information helpful.

Yours sincerely

Rachel Harris
Rachel Harris
Customer Services
C454

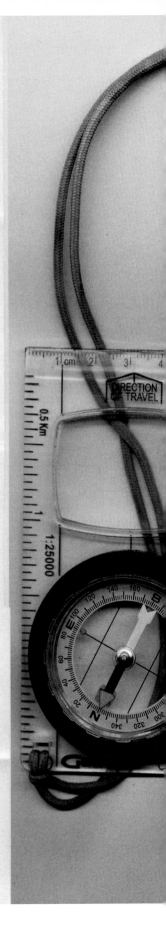

News gaffe 'expert' was IT job candidate

BY FINIAN DAVERN

IT'S not often job candidates can expect to see their performance beamed to the nation live on TV.

But 'an expert' who appeared by mistake on BBC News 24 was actually there for a high-level job interview in the corporation's IT department, it transpired yesterday.

He went along with the whole mix-up because he thought he was being subjected to a new fangled, if odd, initiation exercise.

The would-be BBC employee – Congolese business graduate and IT data cleansing expert Guy Goma – appeared on air instead of his near(ish) namesake Guy Kewney, a journalist, blogger and authority on last week's Apple v

Look-alikes? Guy Goma and Guy Kewney (inset)

Apple trademark battle. As Mr Kewney waited in reception, Mr Goma fielded questions on the issue, remaining remarkably unflappable. But, as the interview progressed, he started to look around as if something wasn't quite as he expected.

Which was fair enough, as it was just an almighty mix-up by a young producer who had just started a new job on the channel.

The experience was 'very stressful' said Mr Goma, who has told some in the BBC he was 'a little upset no one asked him about his data cleansing experience'.

Once staff realised Mr Goma was there for a job, he was taken off air and whisked away for his real interview. He does not yet know if he has got the post as the interview process is ongoing.

When the story first emerged it was thought Mr Goma was Mr Kewney's taxi driver.

And, luckily, Mr Kewney saw the funny side of the episode.

'After the mix-up, they took me over to Broadcasting House for an interview with Radio 4 and were very nice to me,' he said.

©Metro

If he can get an interview at the BBC, can I?

The Old Rectory, Devon

Andi Ford
BBC HR Direct
Level 10
The Mailbox
Birmingham
B1 1RF

19th May 2006

Dear Andi

I'm the man for your advertised position of the Senior Broadcast Journalist, vacancy number 81873, closing date 26th May. Once successful, I'm very happy to move to the flat safety of Cambridge.

I've read through the job description and know that I can present 'Close Up'. So, let me tell you what you are really looking for. It's not someone who has fronted great things in the past. It's someone who has the potential to deliver now and in the future.

Like Guy Goma, I do not have the precise experience that you can simply 'tick off' to put me on your shortlist. More importantly, and also like Guy, I have the ability to react fast to a dynamic on-air situation in order to create news, to put the BBC in the best possible light and to save the day.

Let me come and show you at interview. This is where it counts. You won't be disappointed.

Kind regards

[signature: John Summers]

John Summers

The Old Rectory, Devon

Andi Ford
BBC HR Direct
Level 10
The Mailbox
Birmingham
B1 1RF

13th June 2006

Dear Andi

Please can you give me an update as to where we are with my application? I
wrote in about your advertised position for the Senior Broadcast Journalist,
vacancy number 81873, well ahead of the closing date (copy attached).

The thing is, I have a few things coming up and I don't want to be "out of
circulation" when it's interview time. Also please can you clarify if I'm
expected to get myself to Cambridge or Birmingham for the ordeal?

Kind regards

John Summers

BBC Birmingham
Recruitment
Level 10
The Mailbox
Birmingham
B1 1RF

23rd June 2006

John Summers
The Old Rectory
████████
Devon
████

Dear John

REF: 81873 Presenter/Producer, Look East, Close Up, Cambridge

I write in reference to your letter dated the 13th June 2006. Apologises that I never received your first letter.

Unfortunately the BBC only accept application forms for advertised position which can be accessed online at www.bbc.co.uk/jobs

If you are having problems getting access to the online site, please contact London Recruitment on 0870-333-1330 they will help you set up your account.

Hope this helps with future applications.

Kind Regards,

Andi Ford
BBC Recruitment, Birmingham

INVESTOR IN PEOPLE   1

Northwick Park Road, Harrow, Middlesex

The Officer in Waiting
The College of Arms
Queen Victoria Street
London   EC4V 4BT

27th September 2002

Dear Sir

Something seems to be amiss.

I understand that the Union Jack, dating back to 1606, is a superposition of the flags of St Andrew (for Scotland), St George (for England) and St Patrick (for Ireland).

The blue in the Union Jack comes solely from the Scottish saltire. Now here's the strange bit: the blue in the combined flag is rather dark (technically speaking it is Pantone 280) while your blue is either Pantone 300 or the even lighter Pantone 299.

How can this be? Who is right?

Here are some possible explanations:

-    someone, traveling by horse-drawn carriage, lost the specification between Scotland and London and just made up the colour.

-    the saltire used to be as dark as the Union Jack blue but has been bleached over time by the Scottish weather.

-    ICI Paints Division changed your flag colour to promote their excess stocks of light blue paint.

What is the truth and who is right? Someone is waving the wrong flag and we need to sort it out. I look forward to your answer as I have been told that you are the man who knows.

Kind regards

John Summers

H. E. Paston-Bedingfeld
York Herald

The College of Arms
Queen Victoria Street
London EC4V 4BT
Tel.: (020) 7236 6420
Fax.: (020) 7248 4707
email:ykherald@globalnet.co.uk

Mr John Summers
▮ Northwick Park Road
Harrow
Middlesex, HA1 2NY

24th October 2002

Dear Mr Summers,

Thank you for your letter of 27th September which I received as the Officer in Waiting.

I am afraid to say that our artists do not know Pantone numbers and nor do we as Officers of Arms. Blue is to us simply blue and it should not be too light nor too dark.

I believe this answers your question.

Yours sincerely,

York Herald

Northwick Park Road, Harrow, Middlesex

Noel Brock
Customer Service Manager
Driver and Vehicle Licensing Centre
Longview Road
Morriston
Swansea
South Wales
SA6 7JL

9th September 2002

Dear Mr Brock

Congratulations! You have been selected to participate in the British Customer
Responsiveness Survey, 2002.

Please can you answer these simple questions? What colour of hair should a
bald man enter on his driving licence? And what about a woman who has given
herself a purple rinse, but just for the summer?

If you would like further information on the results of this important national
survey then please let me know.

I look forward to hearing from you.

Kind regards

John Summers

Driver and Vehicle Licensing Agency
Customer Enquiries Drivers
Longview Road
Swansea
SA6 7JL

Mr J Summers
■ Northwich Park Road
Harrow
Middlesex
HA1 2NY

Telephone	01792 ■■■
Fax	01792 ■■■
GTN	1213 8597
Email	
Web Site	http://www.dvla.gov.uk
Minicom	01792 782787

Your reference:
Our reference: CED/LED

Date: 12 September 2002

Dear Mr Summers

Thank you for your letter of 9th September addressed to Mr Noel Brock referring to a British Customer Responsiveness Survey and seeking guidance about declaring hair colour for driving licence purposes. Your letter has been passed to me for reply.

There is no requirement for either a man or a woman to declare their hair colour on a driving licence or any application forms appertaining to driving licences.

I hope you find this information useful.

Thank you for the offer to let us know the result of the survey, however that information is not required.

Yours sincerely

Mrs L Scott Davies
Customer Enquiries Drivers

INVESTOR IN PEOPLE

12/09/02   An executive agency of the Department for Transport

Northwick Park Road

Mrs Lesley Lee
Consumer Services Manager
KitKat
PO Box 203
York
YO91 1XY

9th September 2002

Dear Mrs Lee

Congratulations! You have been selected to participate in the British Customer Responsiveness Survey, 2002.

Please can you answer these simple questions? How many KitKats do I have to buy in order to guarantee that I win your £10,000 Terry Venables prize? I have bought 18 so far.

Secondly, you have written the following "interesting fact" inside one of the wrappers: "Terry Venables is the only England player to have been capped at every level." Please can you explain to me why you consider this to be interesting?

If you would like further information on the results of this important national survey then please let me know.

I look forward to hearing from you.

Kind regards

John Summers

Nestlé UK Ltd

YORK YO91 1XY

TELEPHONE (01904) 604604
FACSIMILE (01904) 604534

www.nestle.co.uk

Mr John Summers
Northwick Park Road
HARROW
Middlesex
HA1 2NY

DIRECT LINE: 0800 000030

DIRECT FAX (01904) 603461

YOUR REF.	0951821A	12 September 2002
	OUR REF.	DATE

Dear Mr Summers

Thank you for your recent letter concerning the Terry Venables Football Chocolate Promotion.

This promotion features on a wide range of our confectionery products, on approximately 70 million bars in total, with an even distribution of the prizes across the brands, throughout the length of the promotion and across the country. There are 10 top prizes of up to £10,000 to be won, and 3,000 prizes of £10. To guarantee winning a top prize with a Kit Kat purchase, you would have to buy all the promotional Kit Kat stock!! Only one of the top £10,000 prizes has been claimed so far (found on Yorkie), so there are still 9 prizes to be found.

The facts printed on the wrappers, grouped into the three categories of chocolate, football and Terry Venables, were compiled to fit in with the theme of the promotion. We recognise that some people will not find all the facts interesting, and are sorry if you have been disappointed by any of them.

Thank you once again for taking the trouble to contact us. I hope that this letter answers your questions and that you will continue to enjoy our products in the future.

Yours sincerely

P. Stephenson

Penny Stephenson
Call Centre Officer
Consumer Services

Northwick Park Road, Harrow, Middlesex

Richard Barrett
Director, UK Service Centre
Fidelity Investment Services Ltd
Oakhill House
130 Tonbridge Rd
Hildenborough
Tonbridge
Kent
TN11 9DZ

17th October 2002

Dear Mr Barrett

I wrote to you last month (letter attached) as part of the British Customer Responsiveness Survey, 2002. So far I have not received your reply. Don't worry – you're not the only company trailing in the results table!

Please can you answer these simple questions? Why is it that the person who invests all of our money is called a broker? Is it to protect you when your funds make a loss!?

Also, now that you are on the second round of this research, what proportion of your correspondence is turned around in more than 5 weeks?

I look forward to hearing from you.

Kind regards

John Summers

Fidelity Investments®

Our reference: TI W002155-221002

Oakhill House
130 Tonbridge Road
Hildenborough
Tonbridge, Kent TN11 9DZ

Telephone: (01732) 361144
Fax: (01732) 838886

22 October 2002

Mr. John Summers
Northwick Park Road
Harrow
Middlesex
HA1 2NY

Dear Mr Summers

British Customer Response Survey

Thank you for your letter dated 17 October 2002, in which you request clarification of the terminology used by Fidelity and also information on our service standards. Please accept my apologies that you did not receive a reply to your letter dated 9 September 2002.

At Fidelity we use the term Broker in the same context as Financial Advisor; someone who advises a client which financial product or service is most suited to his or her requests. The advisor also brokers deals between Fidelity and his clients, hence we refer to them as 'brokers'.

Independent financial advisors are in no way tied to Fidelity, the advice they provide is, as the name suggests, entirely independent. Information passed on to clients by advisors or brokers is based on their own research and they are not in business to protect investment managers who operate underperforming portfolios.

At Fidelity we strive to respond to all queries as soon as possible which means providing a same day turn around to correspondence wherever possible. There are certain points during the course of the year where volumes may prevent an immediate response to an issue (such as towards the end of the tax year). However, we do adjust staffing levels at these times to ensure that clients experience the minimum delay possible.

If you require any more help or information, please contact me on 0800 222   . My extension number is   and I am available Monday to Friday from 9am to 6pm. If for any reason I am away from my desk, please feel free to leave a message and I will endeavour to contact you as soon as possible.

Yours sincerely

Tom Ibbotson
Customer Relations Executive

Northwick Park Road, Harrow, Middlesex

Mrs L McSetridge
Consumer Services Manager
Tetley GB Ltd
Freepost HA4 175
325 Oldfield Lane North
Greenford
Middlesex
UB6 0AZ

10th December 2002

Dear Mrs McSetridge

Congratulations! You have been selected to participate in the last round of the
British Customer Responsiveness Survey, 2002.

Please can you answer these simple questions? What proportion of your
employees take coffee breaks? Are they allowed to mix with tea drinkers or do
you have a policy of strict segregation?

Finally, now that you are on the last round of this research, what proportion of
your correspondence is turned around in more than 3 months?

As I understand that you have a lot of things on your plate (or in your cup), I
enclose £5 towards the administration of your reply.

Kind regards

John Summers

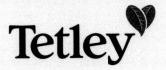

Tetley

11/12/02

Our Ref: 5894811057

Mr Summers
▮ Northwick Park Road
Harrow
Middx
HA1 2NY

Dear Mr Summers

Thank you for your recent letter regarding your British Customer Responsiveness Survey 2002.

As we are unable to participate in this survey, I am returning your £5.00 herewith by Special Delivery. I would like to thank you however for your interest in Tetley.

Yours sincerely

Liane Mcfetridge
Liane Mcfetridge
Consumer Services Manager

THE TETLEY GROUP LIMITED
325 OLDFIELD LANE NORTH, GREENFORD, MIDDLESEX, UB6 0AZ, UK. TELEPHONE: +44 (0)20 8338 4000 www.tetley.com
Registered in England No.3007544 Registered Office 325 Oldfield Lane North, Greenford, Middlesex, UB6 0AZ

PRINTED ON RECYCLED PAPER

105

Northwick Park Road, Harrow, Middlesex

Sir Richard Branson
Virgin Management Limited
120 Campden Hill Road
London
W8 7AR

19th July 2002

Dear Sir Richard

I am conducting a survey among Britain's top CEOs. With 43 companies
spanning bikes to brides and cosmetics to condoms, not to mention your
leading share in the international hot air balloon experience sector, you
certainly qualify for that!

These days it seems that the action of writing to a particular person in a
company almost guarantees that a different person will write back. I wonder if
this is true in Virgin's case?

Keep up the good work and I'll keep up with your Mates!

I look forward to hearing from you.

Kind regards

John Summers

P.S. Other CEO's make it particularly hard to find their names and addresses.
You seem to make it very easy. Is this because they all have something to
hide? Why don't you have something to hide?

Virgin Management Ltd.

Our ref. Rb/080502/ff

5 August 2002

John Summers
 Northwick Park Road
Harrow
Middlesex
HA1 2NY

Dear John,

I wanted to write and thank you for your letter and kind words of support.   It is very much appreciated.

I wish you the best of luck with it all.

Kind regards,

pp Richard Branson
Chairman
Virgin Group of Companies

(Dictated by Richard Branson and signed in his absence)

120 Campden Hill Road | London | W8 7AR | t 020 7313 2000 | f 020 7313 2037

Registered office: 120 Campden Hill Road, London, W8 7AR. Registered in England No.1568894.

Northwick Park Road, Harrow, Middlesex

Brian Buchan, CEO
SSL International plc
Toft Hall
Knutsford
Cheshire   WA16 9PD

9th September 2002

Dear Mr Buchan

Your invitation to participate in the first round of the British CEO Responsiveness Survey (2002) was sent out on July 19th. I thought that you would like to see some of the results. Don't worry, you're not alone at the bottom of the list!

Company	Qualifying Features	Response Time	Comments
ICI	£6.43 B turnover, 38,600 employees, leading share in emulsion one-coat paint sector	4 days	Reply from CEO's PA
Railtrack	£2.5 B turnover, unrivalled collection of level crossings and viaducts, direct access to PM	13 days	CEO away or would have written himself
Virgin	43 companies spanning bikes to brides and cosmetics to condoms	17 days	Dictated by CEO Very upbeat
BNFL	£2.146 B turnover, 23,000 employees, leading share in nuclear clean-up sector	20 days	Reply from CEO
Albro Windows Ltd	UPVC windows, "top quality by a company that makes the difference", in business for 30 years	> 52 days	
SSL International	£592.4 M turnover, Durex, leading share in global rubber glove market	> 52 days	

What can we learn from this? Larger companies seem to respond much faster than smaller ones. Double glazing companies do not respond within 52 days.

Now you have been selected for the second round of this survey. What percentage of mail addressed directly to you goes unanswered? Is there any relationship between that percentage and the facts that your business has a turnover of £592.4 M and a leading share in the global rubber glove market?

I look forward to hearing from you.

Kind regards

John Summers

35 New Bridge Street
London EC4V 6BW
Tel: 020 7367 5760
Fax: 020 7367 5790

13 September 2002

Mr J Summers
█ Northwick Park Road
Harrow
Middlesex
HA1 2NY

Dear Mr Summers

Here is your answer in person. I normally receive 50-100 pieces of unsolicited mail per week inviting me to participate in surveys, subscribe to the most insightful magazines, attend seminars and hire consultants that will do marvellous things for my business. If you believe you are showered in junk mail, you should try this job! In addition there will be the unsolicited mail that is directly relevant such as questions from investors or issues raised by one of our consumers or trader customers. Unless the mail is directly concerned with our business or one of our products, most will go unanswered. Relevant mail is normally directed to the person in the company who can best answer it.

Yours sincerely

Brian J Buchan
Chief Executive

SSL International plc is
registered in England No. 388828.
Registered Office:
35 New Bridge Street, London, England EC4V 6BW

Northwick Park Road, Harrow, Middlesex

Rt Hon Geoffrey Hoon, MP
Secretary of State for Defence
Old War Office
Whitehall
London
SW1A 2EU

23rd September 2002

Dear Mr Hoon

Please can you clarify at what stage in history a war is transferred from the New War Office to the Old War Office?

I know that a car is declared vintage if it was built between 11th Nov 1918 and 31st Dec 1930. I also know that a wine becomes vintage after a bunch of bucolic old bores declare it to be. So who determines when wars become old?

If we go and fight Iraq, from where will this operation be managed? Is there a Future War Office or a Wars That We Don't Want To Have But Think That We Might Get Dragged Into Office?

Please can you clarify for me. I'm confused.

Kind regards

John Summers

From: Mr D.A Slater, Information (Exploitation) Analysis Branch, incorporating Army Historical Branch.
MINISTRY OF DEFENCE
3-5, Great Scotland Yard, London SW1A 2HW

Telephone	(Direct dial)	0207 218
	(Switchboard)	0207 218
	(Fax)	0207 218

Mr J Summers
█ Northwick Park Road
Harrow
Middlesex
HA1 2NY

Our reference
HB (A) 6/2
Date
21 October 2002

Dear Mr Jones

Thank you for your letter dated 23 September 2002.

Firstly, there is no 'New War Office'. Official matters of defence whether historical, contemporary or future are dealt with by the Ministry of Defence.

Defence matters used to be administered by the Air Ministry (for the Royal Air Force), the Admiralty (for the Royal Navy) and the War Office (for the Army). Each service had its own building. When the three administrations were united on 1 April 1964 to become the Ministry of Defence, the building occupied by the War Office simply became known as the 'Old War Office' or the 'Old War Office Building'.

I hope the above information is of help.

Yours sincerely

D.A Slater
Information (Exploitation)-Analysis
Incorporating Army Historical Branch

111

Northwick Park Road, Harrow, Middlesex

Andrew Higginson
Finance Director
Tesco PLC
Delamare Road
Cheshunt
Hertfordshire
EN8 9SL

SCRUMMY BOSTON BROWNIES

Melt 300g dark choc with 225g butter. Add 3 eggs plus 200g dark sugar. Add 75g self-raising flour, 175g broken walnuts and 200g chopped milk chocolate. Bake at 190°C for 35 – 40 minutes. Mmmm!

28th June 2002

Dear Mr Higginson

I am writing to you as you are the Finance Director so, presumably, you're the person who understands numbers and money.

Please can you tell me how it is that I can go into Tesco and buy 200g of Tesco Dark Chocolate for 69p while a 400g bar is £1.74? In addition, the 400g pack has a huge bit of writing across it that screams "BIGGER PACK £ BETTER VALUE".

Now I am not a Finance Director, and I am sure that you have not personally overseen the pricing of every product in every store (how could you!?), but I know that 2 x 200g @ 69p = £1.38 (I've even checked this on my calculator). So this means I've lost 36p every time that I have bought your larger pack! And I've been doing so for quite a while as it's an essential ingredient in my scrummy Boston Brownie recipe - my kids go crazy for it. You can have the recipe if you'd like.

Anyway I look forward to hearing your explanation as to how the bigger pack is better value.

Kind regards

Jane Summers

Jane Summers

Dark
Chocolate
smooth and rich
plain chocolate

Our Ref: 4319165

8 July 2002

Ms Summers
█ Northwick Park Road
HARROW
Middlesex
HA1 2NY

Customer Service
PO Box 73
Baird Avenue
Dryburgh Industrial Estate
Dundee
DD2 3TN
Freephone   0800 505555

Dear Ms Summers

Thank you for your letter addressed to our Finance Director, to which I have been asked to respond. I was sorry to learn of your disappointment with the price of Tesco Dark Chocolate.

I have contacted out stock control department who have advised me that the normal price of the Tesco Dark Chocolate 200g pack is .92p, however, this has recently been on offer at .69p. As this promotion has now finished, the 200g pack has reverted to the normal retailing price of .92p.

It has always been our policy to offer good value to our customers, giving quality products at reasonable prices. However, it can be misleading to look at the prices of only selected products, and we are confident that we do offer products at competitive prices, giving value for money across the whole of our range.

Our Buyers will continue to negotiate the best price possible, and if we obtain any price reductions we will pass them on to our customers immediately.

Thank you for your letter.

Yours sincerely
For and on behalf of Tesco Stores Ltd

Geraldine Martin
Customer Service Manager

Edmunds Gardens, Booker, High Wycombe, Buckinghamshire

Customer Service Manager
Procter & Gamble Ltd
Newcastle-Upon-Tyne
NE99 1EL

3rd May 1991

Dear Sir

I wish to complain about your Ariel product. I was following advice from your very interesting advert on the local radio station (I think it was Capital).

The radio said that there was "one vital component missing from my hoover". I had always thought that it wasn't working as well as it could so I was pleased to hear what you had to say. You said that I should use Ariel with my hoover. I poured a few cupfuls over my dining room carpet and then started to hoover. Unfortunately it didn't really pick up the powder and then the hoover became all clogged up. I went to get a screwdriver to clear the blockage but when I was out of the room my pet dog, Spike, came in and ate some of the powder. He was sick immediately on the carpet and so I had even more mess to clear up.

I think you need to stick to cleaning clothes with Ariel. You should test it more properly before telling me to try it on carpets. Are you just trying to copy those Persil people who think that it can clean plates? Why have you all gone so crazy?

Spike is OK now although I thought he would be blowing bubbles.

Please can you give me better advice in the future?

Kind regards

Jane Summers

Jane Summers

PROCTER & GAMBLE LIMITED

P.O. BOX 1EL, NEW SANDGATE HOUSE, CITY ROAD, NEWCASTLE UPON TYNE, NE99 1EL. TELEPHONE: (091) 235 4000. TELEX: 53311. FAX: (091) 235 4219.

23rd May 1991
Our ref Ariel

Ms. J. Summers,
⬛ Edmunds Gardens,
Booker,
HIGH WYCOMBE,
Bucks. HP12 4LP.

Dear Ms. Summers,

Thank you for your letter from which we were sorry to learn of your unfortunate experience when you mistakenly thought you should use Ariel with your Hoover vacuum cleaner.

Ariel of course is a weekly wash powder and is designed for use in washing machines and to handwash clothes. It is not designed for cleaning carpets.

Our radio advertisement for Ariel was recommending the product for use in washing machines and we are sorry that you misinterpreted the advertisement. We would mention that we have received no similar complaints to your own.

We hope that your dog has now fully recovered from the incident and we are pleased to be able to reassure you that no significant harm can have been caused by your dog eating some of the powder. Like all our products Ariel has been thoroughly tested to ensure that it is safe not only in normal conditions of use but also in the case of accidental ingestion.

Thank you again for contacting us and as a gesture of goowill in this matter we are enclosing a voucher which you can use towards the cost of any of our products the next time you shop.

Yours sincerely,

(Mrs.) Sheila Cassidy
<u>CONSUMER SERVICE DEPARTMENT</u>

COMPANY REGISTERED IN ENGLAND, REG. No. 83758. REGISTERED OFFICE: HEDLEY HOUSE, ST. NICHOLAS AVE, GOSFORTH, NEWCASTLE UPON TYNE, NE99 1EE.
♻ 100% RECYCLED PAPER

Shipton Bellinger, Tidworth, Hampshire

The Complaints Department
Lever Brothers
Kingston-Upon-Thames
Surrey
KT1 2BA

23rd April 1990

Dear Sir

I am worried about your new product Radion because my friends say that it contains the gas Radon that they mention in the news a lot. I am sure that it is safe really but isn't there a risk of danger?

I have also heard that the box is bright orange because of the radioactive Radon. Is this true? I think you should tell us if you are using nasty methods to kill those smelly bugs.

Kind regards

Jane Summers

BY APPOINTMENT
TO H.M. THE QUEEN
SOAP AND DETERGENT MAKERS
LEVER BROTHERS LIMITED
KINGSTON UPON THAMES
SURREY

Our ref:

Your ref:

FP/jh

Personal no: 01-541 8496

Date:

2nd May 1990

Lever Brothers Limited
Lever House 3 St James's Road
Kingston upon Thames
Surrey KT1 2BA
England
Telephone 01-541 8200
Telex 928893

Ms Jane Summers

Shipton Bellinger
Tidworth
Hants

Dear Ms Summers

Thank you for your letter.

We would advise that the Radion packaging has been designed to make an
impact and is more dramatic and "eye catching" than perhaps the majority
of Lever Bros. products.

Extensive consumer market tests were carried out and no problems were
expereinced regarding consumers perceptions of the products value and
quality.

The packaging is standard across Europe and has been so for several
years. Orange was chosen for impact as the majority of washing powders
are packaged in white.

The name Radion was chosen after considerable thought because of its
effectiveness in helping to convey the high technology and scientific
sophisticated nature of the product. We would assure you that there is
no connection with Radiation whatsoever.

We are enclosing a sample of Radion Automatic for you to try and we hope
you will find it lives up to our claims.

Yours sincerely

Jenny Haughton
p.p. F PLATT (MISS)
CONSUMER SERVICE

W1890xo42

Registered in London No. 334527
Registered Office
3 St James's Road
Kingston upon Thames
Surrey KT1 2BA

The Old Rectory, Devon

Patrick Cescau
Group Chief Executive
Unilever plc
Blackfriars
EC4Y 0JP

12th June 2006

Dear Mr Cescau

I've read about the Unilever Series of sponsored art thingies at the Tate
Modern. And I've read that your sponsorship "adds vitality to people's
everyday lives."

But I just don't get it.

The current 'thingy' is a wall of sound – a right mix-up of voices making no
particular sense at all (if you want my opinion!) And the previous 'thingy' was
a huge pile of boxes. That was it.

I don't know if Unilever does much market research but I'd say that all I have
now is more confusion, ear-ache and mystification. Not vitality. Perhaps I just
don't have the right sort of everyday life? Please tell me what I'm meant to
think.

Kind regards

John Summers

Unilever House
Blackfriars
London EC4P 4BQ

T: +44 (0)20 7822
F: +44 (0)20 7822

Mr John Summers
The Old Rectory

Devon

Patrick Cescau
Group Chief Executive

3rd July 2006

Dear Mr Summers

I write in response to your recent letter concerning the Unilever Series at the Tate Modern.

It is certainly not for me to tell you what to think about art. What I can tell you is that the sponsorship has been a great success and has helped to strengthen Unilever's reputation in the UK.

Kind regards

Unilever PLC
Registered in London number 41424
Registered office Port Sunlight,
Wirral, Merseyside CH62 4UJ

The Old Rectory, Devon

The Consumer Relations Manager
Procter & Gamble Ltd
Cobalt 12
Cobalt Business Park
Silver Fox Way
NE27 0QW

22nd May 2006

Dear Sir or Madam

Is your Ariel washing powder still concentrated? Many years ago it came in big back-breaking boxes. Then it shrunk itself into 'cute' little boxes. Now we seem to be back to the giant sizes again.

So, is the stuff inside concentrated or not? And why are we back into big boxes anyway? Is it your way of helping to tackle this country's obesity by making us sweat a bit from the checkout to the car?

What's going on here and when can we look forward to the arrival of concentrated powder once more?

Kind regards

John Summers

Procter & Gamble UK
P.O. Box 420
Newcastle upon Tyne
NE27 0YA
+44 (0) 191 297 8217 phone

www.pg.com

Our ref: 216604
26/05/2006

Mr J Summers
The Old Rectory
⬛⬛⬛⬛⬛
⬛⬛⬛⬛
⬛⬛⬛⬛
United Kingdom

Dear Mr Summers

Thank you for your letter.

I appreciate you taking the time to share your comments with us. This kind of constructive feedback from our consumers is very helpful and I will make sure that your remarks are noted for future reference.

In the hope that you will continue to use our products with confidence, I have enclosed a voucher and some information which can be put toward a future purchase.

Thank you again for taking the time to write to us and for your interest in our product.

Yours sincerely

Penny Harris

Penny Harris
CONSUMER RELATIONS DEPARTMENT

1 CO00107   1 PA001157

A partnership between Procter & Gamble (L&CP) Limited,
and Procter & Gamble (Health & Beauty Care) Limited, The Heights, Brooklands, Weybridge, Surrey, KT13 OXP.

The Old Rectory, Devon

Penny Harris
Consumer Relations Department
Procter & Gamble UK
PO Box 420
Newcastle upon Tyne
NE27 0YA

13th June 2006

Your ref: 216604

Dear Penny

I'm afraid that you haven't answered the questions in my letter dated 22nd May at all. Thanks for the smart voucher though. Unfortunately I have to return this to you as I wouldn't know where to put it on my tax return. Also I enclose 2p to cover the interest that you would have received had you held on to the voucher.

So, back to my questions then ...

Is your Ariel washing powder still concentrated? Many years ago it came in big back-breaking boxes. Then it shrunk itself into 'cute' little boxes. Now we seem to be back to the giant sizes again.

Is the stuff inside concentrated or not? And why are we back into big boxes anyway? Is it your way of helping to tackle this country's obesity by making us sweat from the checkout to the car?

What's going on here and when can we look forward to the arrival of concentrated powder once more?

Kind regards

John Summers

Procter & Gamble UK
P.O. Box 420
Newcastle upon Tyne
NE27 0YA
+44 (0) 191 297 8217 phone

www.pg.com

Our ref: 280158
20/06/2006

Mr J Summers
The Old Rectory

United Kingdom

Dear Mr Summers

Thank you for getting back in touch, and hopefully this letter will answer your query.

Ariel Compact powder was available from 1995 but discontinued in 2001; since then, only standard Ariel powder has been manufactured.

In August 2005, the standard powder was compacted, so less product is now required per wash. We also reduced the size of packaging at that time.

I hope this answers your question, but if you have any further queries or comments please get back in touch with us.

Thank you for your interest in our products.

Yours sincerely

Penny Harris

Penny Harris
CONSUMER RELATIONS DEPARTMENT

A partnership between Procter & Gamble (L&CP) Limited,
and Procter & Gamble (Health & Beauty Care) Limited, The Heights, Brooklands, Weybridge, Surrey, KT13 OXP.

Northwick Park Road, Harrow, Middlesex

Antonia Spanos
General Manager
Dali Universe
County Hall
London
SE1 7PB

10th December 2002

Dear Antonia

Provocative. Insightful. Sensuous. These are some of the words that I would use to describe Dali's works of art in your gallery.

Uncaring. Distracting. Dis-respectful. These are some of the words that I would use to describe the exhibits at the far end of the first corridor.

Why? There you display a Dali quotation:

"Ideas are made to be copied.
I have enough ideas to sell them on.
I prefer that they are stolen so that
I don't have to actually use them myself."

And next to it is a sign:

NO
PHOTOGRAPHS
OR USE OF
VIDEO
EQUIPMENT IS
ALLOWED
IN THE
GALLERY

Why have you over-ruled Dali? Or is this actually in invitation to 'steal' his work by photographing it illegally? I am confused. Please can you clarify what Dali wants, what you want and what I should do to keep you both happy?

As I understand that you are rather busy at the moment, I enclose £5 towards the administration of my reply.

Kind regards

John Summers

John Summers
███ Northwick Park Road
Harrow, Middx
HA1 2NY

16 December 2002

Dear Mr Summers,

Thank you for your letter and for enclosing an administration fee, which I am returning to you.

We are reviewing our signage in January and will take your interesting comments into consideration. As to what Dali himself would want, we presume that it involves maximum exposure for himself and his work...

Thank you for your interest in our gallery, and I take this opportunity to wish you a Merry Christmas.

Kind regards,

Antonia Spanos

County Hall Gallery Ltd., County Hall, Riverside Building, London SE1 7PB
TEL: +44 (0)20 7620 2720   FAX: +44 (0)20 7620 3120   www.daliuniverse.com   email: info@daliuniverse.com
Registered in England No. 03493256   VAT No. 749326407

The Old Rectory, Devon

The Rt Hon Tessa Jowell MP
Department for Culture, Media and Sport
2 - 4 Cockspur Street
London
SW1Y 5DH

13th June 2006

Dear Tessa

It's not fair!

Sometimes people in quiet, secluded rural areas depend upon things like the BBC to get them through the long, dark nights of winter. (I'm not saying that this is not fair, although it isn't either.)

And in some places, it is almost impossible to get a decent picture on the TV. Therefore I assume that in these cases, applying our consumer rights, rural people who can't see the BBC clearly only have to pay a proportion of the licence fee. This is much fairer.

The BBC have told me that you will sort this out. Please can you send me any relevant forms for completion before my licence comes up for (partial) renewal?

Kind regards

John Summers

Department for Culture, Media and Sport
Broadcasting Policy Division

2-4 Cockspur Street
London SW1Y 5DH
www.culture.gov.uk

Tel 020 7211 6200

John Summers
The Old Rectory

Devon

Our Ref   45339

14 July 2006

Dear Mr Summers,

Thank you for your letter to Tessa Jowell of 13 June about current digital TV reception and the TV Licence Fee. I have been asked to reply.

I have noted your comments. I hope you will be reassured by the fact that that current UK Digital Terrestrial Television (DTT) coverage is not indicative of how things will be after switchover. At present DTT is available to around 73% of UK households and, whilst we would of course like to extend this level of coverage, it is not possible to extend it significantly beyond present levels without first switching off the analogue transmissions.

After switchover, all transmitters will broadcast digital signals and digital terrestrial coverage will be extended to reach the same level as current analogue coverage, meaning that if you can receive analogue terrestrial broadcasts now, you should be able to receive the digital signals then.

The Government has committed to ensuring that terrestrial analogue broadcasting signals are maintained until everyone who can currently get the main public service broadcasting channels in analogue form (BBC 1 and 2, ITV, Channel 4/S4C and Channel 5) can receive them on digital systems.

Following on from this, we've been informed by engineering sources that terrestrial digital television transmission technology is, in general, more powerful than its analogue predecessor. Therefore, after switchover local coverage should be much improved, giving viewers in your region access to the regional TV services they require.

I have also noted your comments about the level of Licence Fee paid reflecting individuals' BBC reception. However, a television licence is required to install or use a television receiver to watch any television programme service, under the provisions of the Communications Act 2003 and the Communications (Television Licensing) Regulations 2004.

That definition embraces BBC, ITV, Channel 4, S4C, Channel 5 and satellite and cable broadcasters. The principle is that all viewers who watch any United Kingdom television

service should pay a licence fee and that this fee should be used to fund the BBC. The licence fee is therefore a payment for permission to receive television broadcasts and not for the service provided.

It is payable in full irrespective of the use made of that service and the quality of reception. This ensures that, while the television licence remains the principal source of funding for the BBC, the Corporation remains adequately funded, and can provide its full range of television and radio services.

I hope you find this information useful.

Yours sincerely,

Chris Fosten
Central Information and Briefing Unit

127

The Old Rectory, Devon

The Consumer Relations Manager
Ferrero UK Ltd
Awberry Court
Hatters Lane
Croxley Business Park
Watford
Hertfordshire
WD18 8PA

17th May 2006

Dear Sir or Madam

Help!

I've seen one of your adverts for Kinder Eggs. It told me how each egg contains "a toy, a chocolate and a surprise" so I bought one for my daughter. She found the toy and chocolate but not the surprise. It must have been left out so please can you let me know what she should have found inside?

Kind regards

John Summers

FERRERO UK LIMITED

Awberry Court, Hatters Lane, Croxley Business Park, Watford, Herts. WD18 8PA
Telephone: 01923 690300 Fax: 01923 690400

19 May 2006

Mr J Summers
The Old Rectory
████████████
Devon
████████

Dear Mr Summers

I was most concerned to receive your letter regarding a Kinder Surprise which did not
contain a toy. This kind of incident is obviously very disappointing.

Ferrero is one of the largest confectionery manufacturers in the world and the Company
always tries its best to ensure that all its products leave the factory in perfect condition.
We take great pride in the high quality of our products and are always concerned on the
rare occasions when there is a negative incident connected to one of them. Any feedback
from our consumers is of great value to Ferrero as this enables us to make any
improvements that may be necessary.

May I offer you Ferrero's sincere apologies for the disappointment and inconvenience this
has caused and trust you will accept the enclosed Kinder Surprise toys with my
compliments.

Thank you for bringing this matter to our attention.

Yours sincerely

Dorothy Fleri
Consumer Relations Department

Enc

The Old Rectory, Devon

Dorothy Fleri
Consumer Relations Department
Ferrero UK Ltd
Awberry Court
Hatters Lane
Croxley Business Park
Watford
Hertfordshire
WD18 8PA

22nd May 2006

Dear Dorothy

Thank you for your prompt reply dated May 19th. I am returning the toys you sent me, complete with their capsules unopened, as it is against my moral beliefs to accept these gifts from you.

However I am still puzzled as my question has not been answered.

I'm sure your advertisement says that each egg contains "a toy, a chocolate and a surprise". The egg that I bought did contain a toy (a charming little man/woman with a wheelie thing) and, of course, the chocolate but I couldn't find the "surprise". What intrigues me now is where the surprise is meant to fit anyway. There seems to be virtually no space between the toy capsule and the egg. What kind of surprise should my daughter and I have expected? Something small like a diamond!?

Please let me know what we have missed out on.

Kind regards

John Summers

FERRERO

FERRERO UK LIMITED

Awberry Court, Hatters Lane, Croxley Business Park, Watford, Herts. WD18 8PA
Telephone: 01923 690300 Fax: 01923 690400

24 May 2006

Mr J Summers
The Old Rectory

Devon

Dear Mr Summers,

I was concerned to receive your further letter with regard to Kinder Surprise and I am sorry that I misunderstood your previous correspondence, believing you had not received a toy.

The concept of Kinder Surprise is centralised on which toy will be enclosed. We know from years of market research in various countries that boys and girls enjoy making and collecting all the different kinds of toys in Kinder Surprise. We always strive to ensure that the toys have as broad an appeal as possible and the range of over 120 construction and one-piece toys is changed every autumn, offering our customers a constant variety of toys to collect The combination of the two is a response to demand for both types of toys, with construction toys forming over half of the range.

Further to your inquiry regarding the content of the advertisements on the wrappers, I would like to confirm that they state, "contains surprise toy"

Nevertheless any feedback from our consumers is of great value to Ferrero and I am most grateful to you for taking the time and trouble to write to us with your comments, which I will certainly pass on to our Kinder Surprise department.

Yours sincerely

Dorothy Fleri
Consumer Relations Department

Registered in England. Registration No. 876127

Northwick Park Road, Harrow, Middlesex

Louise Johnson
London Transport Museum
Covent Garden Piazza
London
WC2E 7BB

13th June 2002

Dear Louise

Why have you put up that poster on the underground!? The one that says:

> *"Before they invented engines, a 1000 tonnes of horse dung were dropped on the streets of London every day. Who cleaned it up?"*

If you don't know the answer then what makes you think that anyone else will know? And why do you want to know the answer to this obscure question anyway?

Here is a £5 contribution towards the cost of putting up some more attractive posters. If I can cast my vote, I'd like to see more pictures of good quality home cooking so that I can start to dream about going home in the evenings. This would be a much more inviting image to conjure up on the Underground. Horse pooh – no! Good home cooking – yes!

I look forward to hearing your point of view on the poster.

Kind regards

Jane Summers

Jane Summers

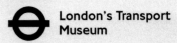
Ms Jane Summers
Northwick Park Road
Harrow
Middlesex
HA1 2NY

18 June 2002

Dear Ms Summers

Thank you for your letter dated 13 June 2002 about our latest poster campaign.
We greatly appreciate feedback from members of the public and your comments
were interesting to us.

Our research for this year's campaign resulted in six ideas being put to various
groups for consideration. Three of these six ideas were chosen to become the final
posters. I am sure you will also have seen the 'Not just 4 anoraks' poster and the
endearing image of a couple reminiscing about their early dates on an old bus. The
idea for 'How much poo is that?' came from the most commonly asked question by
children who visit the museum. I am sure you are aware if you have children of your
own, their fascination with bodily functions leads to them asking all sorts of related
questions!

The question asked in the poster 'Who cleaned it up?' relates to the vast resource
of social history at the Museum, much of which refers to transport staff
themselves, including Victorian street cleaners. One of the most popular Museum
actors is a Victorian passenger who explains her disgust at the state of Victorian
streets, which plays a significant part in the development of the London transport
story. She also tells the story of the orphans and street urchins who were paid
small sums to clear manure from public crossways.

Please find enclosed the five pound note you kindly sent to us together with a
complimentary ticket for you and a friend to visit to the Museum and learn more
about the many characters who played a part in the history of transport in London.

With kind regards

Yours sincerely

Claire Ingham
Claire Ingham
Head of Marketing

INVESTOR IN PEOPLE

Designated as a museum with an
outstanding collection

London's Transport Museum, Covent Garden, London WC2E 7BB
Telephone 020 7379 6344, Fax 020 7565 7254, Internet www.ltmuseum.co.uk

Registered office: Windsor House, 42-50 Victoria Street, London SW1H 0TL, Registered in England and Wales, Company Number 3914810, VAT Number 756 2770 08

London's Transport Museum is a division of Transport Trading Limited

Northwick Park Road, Harrow, Middlesex

Debbie Gearing
Brand Manager
Lipton Tea
Brooke House
Manor Royal Crawley
West Sussex
RH10 9SD

16th July 2002

Re: Big Pants

Dear Debbie

I am intrigued by your Big Pants poster for Lipton Ice Tea. You see, I have actually gone out and bought your drink, but here's where it all goes a bit wrong in my opinion. When I tried to drink the tea, I couldn't help but think about that large pair of pants. And, if I may be so bold as to share my thoughts, the fact that your drink is a similar colour to marks that one might find on a pair of big pants does nothing to warm me to your iced product.

I have an idea. Please can you send me a small copy of your Big Pants poster? Here's why. Next time I go to see Tom Jones in concert (he usually does something before Christmas), I will quite happily wave a copy of your poster at him. I know he loves being mobbed by ladies' undergarments, be they large or small.

I look forward to receiving a copy of your poster.

Kind regards

Jane Summers

Unilever

Unilever Bestfoods *UK*

Brooke House Manor Royal Crawley West Sussex RH10 9RQ
Telephone 01293 648000

Direct line 01293

Facsimile 01293

24th July 2002

Dear Jane
Re: Big Pants
I am just writing to thank you for your letter. Please find enclosed a copy of the Big Pants ad for you to wave at the next Tom Jones concert.

To overcome the problem you are having with images of soiled pants, I have also included another of our ad executions so that hopefully you may get somewhat different associations next time you drink Lipton Ice Tea.

Many thanks for your interest, custom and the entertainment your letter has given us.

Kind regards,

Peter Baxendell
Lipton Ice Tea UK Business Manager

Unilever Bestfoods UK is the trading name of Van den Bergh Foo...
Registered office Brooke House Manor ...

Northwick Park Road, Harrow, Middlesex

Tom Jones
c/o Gut Records
PO Box 9214
London
W9 2BR

16th July 2002

Dear Tom

I have seen a poster with a picture of Big Pants. It is trying to persuade me to drink a brand of iced tea. It's a strange image to put out at me! I bet even you would be a little dismayed if someone threw such a large pair at you!

Out of interest, what is the most unusual item of ladies' undergarment that has ever had the good fortune to be thrown at you? Certainly I don't think you'd be very interested in receiving mine – they'd knock you out!

Please can you send me a signed photo of yourself? Fully-clothed will do just fine! (Are your Welsh fans as reserved as us prim English?)

I look forward to your friendly photo.

Kind regards

Jane Summers

TOM JONES

Dear Jane,

Thank you very much for your letter and for being in touch. I really do appreciate your kind comments and your support, as do my band, crew and management staff. It is important that we all get feedback from those who enjoy some part of what I do, so thanks again for making the effort.

Last year, 2001, was an excellent time with successful tours in Europe, California, the UK and Eastern Europe and Russia. I also started recording my second album for Gut Records, which will follow the highly successful *Reload* album released at the end of 1999. The project is not a follow-up 'duets' album—it will be different, and I'm working with some very interesting producers, including the wonderful Wyclef Jean for several tracks. We'll hopefully have a release in summer 2002, and I'm really looking forward to that.

We've also filmed a live show that was done in Cardiff, So. Wales, UK, last summer. It's a great performance, so keep an eye out for a broadcast on a station in your area sometime soon. An extended v⋯ ⋯f this concert, plus extra footage of other performances and items, shoul⋯ ⋯⋯ later in 2002.

I'll also be developing my ow⋯ via the Gut Records site, or b⋯

Tom Jones Enterpris⋯
10100 Santa Monic⋯
Los Angeles, CA ⋯
310-552-0044

Valley Music Ltd⋯
11 Cedar Court,
Fairmile,
Henley on Than⋯
Oxon, RG9 2J⋯
+44-(0)1491-8⋯

Thanks very much! ⋯

BEST WISHES
Tom Jones

Northwick Park Road, Harrow, Middlesex

Andy Parfitt
Radio 1 Newsdesk
BBC
Broadcasting House
Wood Lane
W1A 1AA

17th May 2002

Dear Andy,

I've just heard a news bulletin on Radio 1 (it was at 10:30 this morning) where you mentioned some research that had been carried out by the RAC. You reported that, according to their research, the British public want to pay less for petrol. In addition, they want public transport services to improve.

Without wishing to sound rude, I wonder what results they were expecting from this research!? Who wouldn't want cheaper petrol and better public transport? Therefore please can you tell me why this was covered as part of a news item? It seems to me that the only real story here is the fact that the RAC are wasting their money on finding out something that we know already. Next they'll be telling us that they've 'discovered' most cars have four wheels!

Finally what do you think it says about your audience if you are broadcasting this sort of news!?

It has occurred to me that this problem may have arisen because you are underfunded. With this in mind, I enclose £5 as a contribution towards your programme running costs.

I look forward to your reply with anticipation.

Kind regards

John Summers

From Controller, Radio 1

John Summers
█ Northwick Park Road
Harrow
Middlesex
HA1 2NY

24 May 2002

Dear John

Thanks so much for your letter. Please find a returned £5 – funding is modest for what we achieve for the UK's young people, but well managed, and I would hate to deprive you of your hard earned. I will pass your note on to our News Editor, the RAC story does sound like crap.

With thanks

Andy Parfitt
Controller Radio1 & 1Xtra

PS We are about to commission and in-depth documentary based on your idea that most cars have four wheels – is this plagiarism?

1

Northwick Park Road, Harrow, Middlesex

Stuart Mahoney
Customer Acquisitions Manager
The AA
Southwood East
Apollo Rise
Farnborough
GU14 0JW

28th June 2002

Dear Mr Mahoney,

I have written to the RAC questioning some rather strange market research that they have publicised. However they have not replied to me as yet!

I wonder what the AA would do in this situation? Is it correct to equate an inability to reply with an inability to answer a breakdown call?

Here is what I wrote to them about. I heard a news bulletin on Radio 1 where it was reported that, according to the RAC's research, the British public want to pay less for petrol. In addition, they want public transport services to improve. So I asked the RAC why they commissioned this piece of unsurprising research.

Just to satisfy my curiosity, has the AA ever 'discovered' such things in research?

Please find enclosed £5 as a contribution towards the administration costs of your fine organisation.

I look forward to hearing from you soon.

Kind regards

John Summers

The Automobile Association

The Automobile Association Limited
Norfolk House, Priestley Road
Basingstoke, Hampshire RG24 9NY

30 July 2002

John Summers
■ Northwick Park Road
Harrow
Middlesex
HA1 2NY

Dear Mr Summers

Thank you for your letter and kind contribution to our administrative costs. We hardly deserve it taking so long to reply – but we have just moved and are still sorting out the packing cases!

I am enclosing some reports which I hope are of general interest. We are currently planning to update our research on attitudes to road charging. I have enclosed the results from a survey we undertook last autumn regarding congestion charging.

The AA has been arguing for some time for the complete reform of motoring taxation and the way we pay for roads and local transport. The trouble is that people won't buy into any new system of pay as you go until trust is restored. The motoring public have good reason to be sceptical.

Thank you for getting in touch.

Yours sincerely

[signature]

Paul Watters
Head of Roads and Transport Policy
Motoring Policy Unit
Telephone: 01256 ■■■■■
www.aapolicy.com

AA Foundation for Road Safety Research

Ruth Bridger
Company Secretary

5 July 2002

John Summers
25 Northwick Park Road
Harrow
Middlesex
HA1 2NY

Tel: +44 1256 494414 Fax: +44 1256 492092
Email: ■■■■■@theaa.com

RECEIPT

Receipt Date: 3 July 2002

Details of goods and services
Cash received with thanks

	Amount
	£5.00
Total	
	£5.00

Northwick Park Road, Harrow, Middlesex

The Parking Fines Supervisor
London Borough of Harrow
PO Box 951
Civic Centre
Harrow
HA1 2FY

22nd July 2002

Dear Sir / Madam

Thank you for the parking ticket which was applied to my windscreen by Attendant No. 66. Do you have a number as well?

I am amazed that I have been fined for parking in what appears to be the incorrect place. I have lived in Harrow for many years yet have never made a mistake. Indeed you have just put a zoned parking area on my road and so I believe that I know the rules.

Yesterday, on Sunday afternoon, I went swimming. The swimming pool carpark was full due to a Hindu function. So I parked on the road. Knowing that it was Sunday afternoon, I 'knew' that it was OK.

When I came out of the pool I saw a ticket on my window. I thought it was a joke! But it's not (is it?)

So, grudgingly, here is my cheque. But I wish to appeal against the unfairness of this system. If the roads near to the swimming pool have special restrictions, as seems to be the case, why don't you provide a helpful sign saying "Unlike the other Harrow schemes, don't even dare to park here at any time unless you have a resident's permit". A simple fix and we'd all be happy.

In fact I enclose an extra pound towards the printing of suc⬛

Kind regards

John Summers
Member of the General Public No.1

LONDON BOROUGH OF HARROW
P.O. Box No. 951, Civic Centre, Harrow, HA1 2FY

Road Traffic Regulation Act 1984
Road Traffic Act 1991, Section 66 and Schedule 6 (as amended)

Penalty Charge Notice: HR18570046

VRM   : ⬛⬛⬛⬛⬛
Make   : VOLVO
Colour : SILVER

Seen at:
CHRISTCHURCH AVE CHRISTCHURCH-BYRO

Location:
OS 225

On   : 21/07/02
Issue Time : 15:26

By Parking Attendant No: 66

Who had reasonable ca⬛

LONDON BOROUGH OF HARROW
ENVIRONMENTAL SERVICES

P.O. Box 951
Civic Centre
Harrow
Middlesex
HA1 2FY

Switchboard: 020 8863 5611
Direct Line: 020 8424 ▓▓▓
Fax: 020 8424 ▓▓▓

ENVIRONMENT&
TRANSPORTATION

Mr J Summers
▓▓ Northwick Park Road
Harrow
Middx
HA1 2NY

7th November 2002

Dear Mr Summers

Penalty charge notice: HR18570046

I am writing in reply to your letter dated 8th October 2002, addressed to Mrs Vary. I note that you are querying why you have not received a reply to your earlier letter dated 22nd July 2002. Our records show that you enclosed a cheque with that letter to pay the outstanding charge and the above penalty charge was paid in full on 14th August 2002.

Making full payment of the penalty charge normally removes the right to appeal. For that reason the Council does not usually enter into any further correspondence with the motorist subsequent to payment being received. A motorist cannot pay at the discounted level **and** appeal. Payment at the discounted rate is provided by the legislation for those motorists who accept that the parking ticket has been correctly issued and simply wish to discharge their liability within 14 days of the date of issue of the parking ticket.

Having reviewed your circumstances it is not considered there are any grounds to justify cancelling the penalty charge notice, but if you wish to make formal representations or appeal to the Independent Adjudicator I am prepared to refund your payment so that you may do so. However, in the event of your appeal's refusal, payment of the full penalty charge of £60 will be due. Please indicate if this is your intention within 14 days of the date of this letter.

Regarding the times of the restriction of the resident's bays in Christchurch Avenue. The area in which you were parked is designated a Controlled Parking Zone. This is marked by large signs at all points of entry and yellow lines; resident's bays are also marked out and should not be used by anyone other than permit holders for that zone during the restricted times. In this case the times of restriction are between 7 a.m. and Midnight, Monday to Sunday inclusive. The times of restrictions vary between Controlled Parking Zones, as there are local considerations to be taken into account when deciding the restricted times. The method of signing the restriction is in accordance with the Traffic Signs Regulations and General Directions Act 1994.

I trust this has explained the Council's position

Yours sincerely

Stewart Brown
Customer Service Manager-Parking Enforcement

INVESTOR IN PEOPLE

143

Northwick Park Road, Harrow, Middlesex

Dennis Thompson
Parking and Enforcement Officer
London Borough of Harrow
Civic Centre
HA1 2UZ

11th June 2002

Dear Mr Thompson

There is a problem. Please can you tell me what to do?

Often I have to drive my car on the road that goes behind the Council offices.
But it's always blocked ... by council cars! In fact I don't think that it is
possible to be legal and to use this road to travel northwards.

Let me explain.

As you'll see from the enclosed photo, there are cars parked on the northbound
side but it is not possible to pass them without crossing into the part of the
road which is marked out with white lines. And I understand that cars are not
allowed to enter this white area. So how can I get past yet remain an honest
citizen!?

Please can you clarify the following:

-   will I be prosecuted if I enter the area marked by white lines?
-   why are council cars allowed to block the road?
-   is it now OK to park on corners and bends?

Kind regards

John Summers

LONDON BOROUGH OF HARROW
ENVIRONMENTAL SERVICES

P.O. Box 38
Civic Centre
Harrow
Middlesex
HA1 2UZ

Telephone: 020 8424 ▓▓
Fax: 020 8424 ▓▓
E-Mail: ▓▓▓▓▓▓▓▓

**ENVIRONMENT
AND
TRANSPORTATION**

Mr John Summers
▓ Northwick Park Road
Harrow
Middx HA1 2NY

The officer dealing with this matter is:-
Mrs A Taylor

Date: 17 June 2002

Our Ref: AT/70.01/13

Dear Mr Summers

Parking in Milton Road

I have been asked to reply to your letter to Dennis Thompson dated 11 June concerning parking and road markings in Milton Road.

Most of the yellow lines in Milton Road restrict parking between 8am and 6.30pm Monday to Saturday. However, because the road is sufficiently wide, and it is considered safe to do so, parking is permitted on the northbound side at off-peak times in the section you have photographed. Here the yellow lines restrict parking in peak periods i.e. between 8am and 9.30am and between 4.30 and 6.30pm Monday to Friday, but at all other times parking is permitted. This road is public highway and as such is available for any vehicle, it is not reserved for Council staff.

As the bend restricts visibility, central hatching has been provided to channel and separate southbound right turning traffic to Poets Way from northbound right turning traffic into the rear of the Civic Centre.

Although it is an offence to enter a hatched area bordered by a solid white line it is a common misconception that it is also an offence to enter an area of cross hatching bordered by broken lines, when in fact it is not. Section 109 of the Highway Code states that you should not enter the area unless it is necessary and you can see that it is safe to do so.

I hope this clarifies the problem for you, but do not hesitate to contact me if I can be of any further assistance.

Yours sincerely

Ann Taylor
Parking Management Officer

Director of Environmental Services: **TREVOR PUGH**
Head of Property and Development: **GEOFF EASTON** BSC ARICS
Head of Environment and Transportation: **BRYNN HODGSON** FRICS DMS
Chief Planning Officer: **GRAHAM JONES** B.Sc (SocSci) DipTP DipUD IHBC MRTPI

INVESTOR IN PEOPLE

Northwick Park Road, Harrow, Middlesex

Ann Taylor
Parking Management Officer
London Borough of Harrow
Civic Centre
HA1 2UZ

24th June 2002

Your ref: AT/70.01/13 – Parking in Milton Road

Dear Mrs Taylor

Thank you for your reply dated June 17th. It is clear that the area of cross hatching bordered by broken lines on Milton Road is causing confusion. However, I think I have a solution, as featured on BBC Radio 4's Today programme today. (When else!?)

A famous traffic consultant, Ben Hamilton-Baillie, has told the Institution of Civil Engineers that road safety could be **improved** by digging up the pavements, removing the traffic signs and wiping out road markings that show the right of way. This rather strange idea is catching on fast in Holland and Denmark, both pioneers of road safety.

Apparently, when all signs of priority are removed from a junction, drivers and pedestrians take more responsibility for their actions. Indeed they make more eye contact to work out who moves next. Some of the latest junctions in northern Europe are being designed along these lines – just a square with no raised pavements and no indication as to who has right of way. It's like returning to the days before the car!

The best bit is that these plans reduce accidents without affecting journey times. So what is Harrow Council's response to this? Will we see a test in our neighbourhood, perhaps even in Milton Road?

Kind regards

John Summers

LONDON BOROUGH OF HARROW
ENVIRONMENTAL SERVICES

P.O. Box 37
Civic Centre
Harrow
Middlesex
HA1 2UY

Telephone: 020 8424 ▇▇▇
Minicom: 020 8424 7501
Fax: 020 8424 ▇▇▇
E-Mail: ▇▇▇▇@harrow.gov.uk

ENVIRONMENT &
TRANSPORTATION

John Summers
▇ Northwick Park Road
Harrow
Middlesex
HA1 2NY

Our ref: MRS/92.05/60

Date: 11th July 2002

Dear Mr Summers

TRAFFIC CONSULTANT. BEN HAMILTON-BAILLIE

Your letter dated 24th June 2002 addressed to Ann Taylor, the Parking Management Officer concerning the above has been passed to me for a response as this matter falls within my responsibility.

As a member of the Institution of Civil Engineers, I am aware of both the presentation to the Institution and the reporting of it, in both the technical press, in some national newspapers and on the radio. I have no doubt that the Department for Transport (DfT) is monitoring the success or otherwise of these experimental schemes being conducted in places such as in the northern Friesland region. The DfT will advise local authorities if they feel that their application could be used here. Primary legislation by the Government would probably be needed before local authorities such as Harrow could introduce such schemes.

In fact the Government and local authorities have been moving in this direction for some time and you may have heard of something called "Homes Zones". These are the equivalent of the Dutch schemes known as "Woonervens". Eight experimental schemes are currently being trialed in England, the nearest being in Ealing. Harrow is actively considering such a scheme for the Rayners Lane Estate and if implemented and successful we shall consider applying this elsewhere.

Part of the concept of Home Zones is to reduce regulatory signage and control to the bare minimum through the design process and to give a higher priority to pedestrians and cyclists rather than traffic. For such schemes to be successful, it is usually necessary to change the layout considerably so as to emphasise that the vehicles no longer have priority.

In addition, for many years local authorities including Harrow have been approving new residential schemes that have shared surfaces i.e. no demarcation between traffic and pedestrians. Usually there are no signs or markings present in such schemes, although one or two have had parking problems rather than safety problems because of this. We shall continue to approve such schemes where this is considered appropriate

Thank you for your interest in the matter.

Yours sincerely

Mike Symons
Principal Engineer, Traffic Management (West)

147

Northwick Park Road, Harrow, Middlesex

Oliver Rudgard
Brand Manager – Adult Impulse Ice-creams
Birds Eye Walls
Station Avenue
Walton On Thames
KT12 1NT

16th July 2002

Dear Oliver

My eye has been rather caught by your poster. I don't know if this is the first complaint that you have received but I'm not particularly happy with the message that you are putting out. It's the one that goes "I'll have all three".

Let me explain. I think it's rather greedy for anyone to consume three of your, let's face it, damnedly delicious ice-creams. And I think that it's even worse for you to suggest to us, the general public, that we should have to have three ice-creams at a go in order to be seen as 'cool' by our peers.

It is particularly important to get this communication right when it comes to today's youth. If a person was to consume all three in one session, I'm sure that they would go way over the recommended daily limit for e-numbers.

So, let's say "no" to session eating of ice-creams and "yes" to moderation.

Please can you give me your assurance that you will recommend more modest consumption in future?

And please can you send me a small copy of your posters?

Kind regards

John Summers

BIRDS EYE WALL'S

working together for the best

Wall's

John Summers
■ Northwick Park Road
Harrow
Middlesex
HA1 2NY

22 July 2002

RE: "Saucy Postcard" Poster Campaign

Dear John

Thank you very much for your recent letter letting us know your views on the current "Saucy Postcard" Poster campaign.

It is always a pleasure when our consumers take the time to write to us and let us know what they think. As such, I can assure you that your comments have been listened to

You mention in your letter that you enjoy eating our "damnedly delicious" ice cream, and as such please enjoy one or two on us this summer!

Unfortunately, we do not have any small copies of the posters that you see, however I enclose a postcard set that replicates the theme of the campaign.

Wishing you a pleasant summer, I hope you continue to enjoy our ice cream!

Yours sincerely,

Christopher Carter
Ice Cream Marketing

Birds Eye Wall's Limited   Station Avenue   Walton on Thames   Su.
Tel (01932) 263000 **Fax** (01932) 263152

Registered Office   Station Avenue   Walton on Thames   Surrey   Registered London 343496   VAT Registered Number GB 211 486 0.

Northwick Park Road, Harrow, Middlesex

Tony McGrath
Marketing Director
Kronenbourg
Scottish Courage Ltd
Fountain House
160 Dundee St
Edinburgh
EH11 1DQ

9th December 2002

Dear Tony

My eye has been rather caught by your excellent poster. It's the one that goes "If Britain were French, this poster wouldn't be censored".

I just wonder whether you really needed to blame the British authorities, by implication, when you decided to cover up part of your image? Just take a look at page three of the Sun and you'll see that they haven't censored anything. And they're not French. In fact they're owned by an Australian. Perhaps that explains it.

So, go on! Be brave! Censor the 'censored' sign and let us all enjoy the wonderful form that is the human body. Unless it turns out that she has a blotchy chest.

Whatever happens next, please can you send me a small copy of the poster? Complete with the 'censored' sign is fine by me. I'm not a pervert!

Kind regards

John Summers

P.S. Is there any way that I can obtain free beer? (My mother always taught me "nothing ventured, nothing gained.")

SCOTTISH COURAGE
— LIMITED —
BREWERS SINCE 1749

27 February 2003

John Summers
█ Northwick Park Road
Harrow
Middlesex
HA1 2NY

Dear Mr Summers,

I am in receipt of your letter to Tony McGrath dated 9th December.

Unfortunately, these posters were done only in a 96-sheet version and we therefore do not have them in a condensed format. We can, however, supply you with a jpeg of this image if you would like to forward your e-mail address to ███████ @scottish-courage.co.uk.

Alternatively, you can log on to the Kronenbourg 1664 website www.k1664.co.uk and download this image for yourself. This will also give you the opportunity to keep your eye on future competitions to win free beer!

Yours sincerely

Ben Jones
BRAND MANAGER

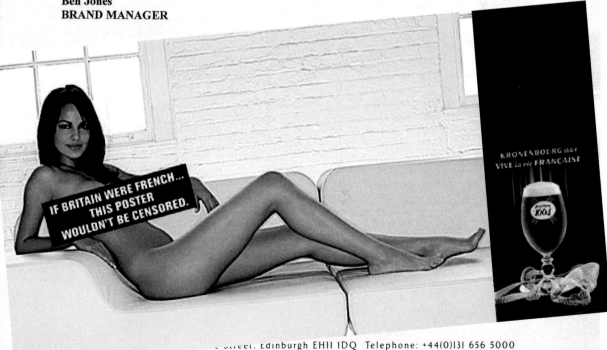

─────── Street. Edinburgh EH11 1DQ Telephone: +44(0)131 656 5000
Registered Office: 33 Ellersly Road Edinburgh EH12 6HX Registered at Edinburgh No. 65527

Northwick Park Road, Harrow, Middlesex

Andrex Customer Services
Kimberly-Clark Limited
1 Tower View
Kings Hill
West Malling
Kent
ME19 4HA

Brown loo paper !?
Think about it ...

8th May 2002

Dear Sir / Madam,

I have just had my husband redecorate our bathroom – he has used a selection of wood finishes, although this was my choice rather than his! I like to have everything matching and so have thrown away our old wedding towels and have purchased some much fluffier brown towels, as well as other bathroom accessories to match our brown bathroom. The thing that annoys me, and it is only a small thing but it does **really** annoy me, is that I can find every other shade of toilet paper apart from brown! I used to buy the pink but it really would not match now and I don't want the toilet paper to stick out from everything else in my bathroom. I haven't spent all that money just to get the details wrong!

So can you recommend a shop where I can buy your brown toilet paper? I'm sure that I can't be alone in wanting it – natural colours are so "in" these days, aren't they?

Please let me know soon as I want to have everything ship-shape before my guests come round.

Kind regards

Jane Summers

Kimberly-Clark

0722517A

13 May 2002

Ms J Summers
Northwick Park Road
HARROW
Middlesex
HA1 2NY

Dear Ms Summers,

Thank you for your recent letter regarding ANDREX® toilet tissue.

I should like to confirm that all the information you have given me has been detailed on our database, this information will now be seen by the Marketing/Quality Manager for this product.

Thank you for taking the time to contact us.

Yours sincerely

Our Ref: 4141650

17 May 2002

Ms Jane Summers
Northwick Park Road
HARROW
Middlesex
HA1 2NY

TESCO

Customer Service
PO Box 73
Baird Avenue
Dryburgh Industrial Estate
Dundee
DD2 3TN
Freephone   0800 505555

Dear Ms Summers

Thank you for your letter received on 17th May, with reference to you asking us to stock brown toilet paper.

Our Buyers decide what our stores sell and I have asked our Buyer for this product range to consider your request. As we stock products according to their popularity and the amount of available space, I cannot say at this stage whether or not we will start selling this product.

Thank you for taking the time and trouble to write to us. We do like to hear from our customers. Your comments and suggestions help us to decide what products we sell and the policies we follow. I hope we may look forward to your continued and valued custom.

Yours sincerely
For and on behalf of Tesco Stores Ltd

Nicola Stewart
Customer Service Manager

Northwick Park Road, Harrow, Middlesex

Dr. Rowan Williams
The Archbishop of Canterbury
Lambeth Palace
London
SE1 7JU

29th August 2002

Dear Dr. Williams

Congratulations on your recent appointment. It's good to have a man at the helm with strong clear opinions.

However, I think that I have found you out. Actually I can't claim the credit. It's all down to my children.

They saw a photo of you (and a remarkably fine one it was too). And immediately they identified you as the Prince of Thieves from Disney's Aladdin. Clearly this is a rather unfortunate double to have. (The Prince is actually the rather unsavory Jafar in disguise.)

When I told my boys that you normally wear a purple cloak, this merely confirmed the fact of your real identity to them.

So, what is the truth? Have you based your physical image on a Disney character or have they based theirs on you?

Please send me a signed photograph so that I can educate them on the differences between you and Jafar.

Kind regards

John Summers

Photo: Eleanor Bentall

For John Summers
with best wishes,
+ Rowan Cantuar:

The Old Rectory, Devon

Census Customer Services
ONS
Titchfield
Fareham
Hants
PO15 5RR

13th June 2006

Dear Sir or Madam

Where are they? I would like to join them in humble supplication but I can't find their places of worship. I am, of course, referring to the dedicated followers of the Jedi Religion.

As I understand it, the UK Census on 29th April 2001 showed that over a million people stated that Jedi was their faith. Exactly how many people owned up to this? And how does this compare to the size of other religions?

Can you help me to find their churches / mosques / synagogues / temples or spaceships as they are eluding me? I have read *The Da Vinci Code* (yes, every single word) and can find no clue as to where Jedis are likely to congregate in devotion. It seems that either they meet under intense secrecy or there has been a state-sponsored crack-down on this religious minority. In either case I'm mystified.

How large is this movement and where are they?

Kind regards

John Summers

John Summers

The Old Rectory

██████████

Devon

██████

Office for **N**ational **S**tatistics (Titchfield)
Census Customer Services
Room 4300S
ONS
Segensworth Road
Titchfield
Fareham
Hants
PO15 5RR

Tel: **01329 813501**
Fax: **01633 652 981**
GTN:
Website: **www.statistics.gov.uk**
Email: **census.customerservices@ons.gov.uk**

15 June 2006

Our Ref:

Your Ref:

Dear Mr Summers

Thank you for your letter of the 13th June 2006.

I have attached two documents which have been copied from the ONS website. The first "390,000 Jedis There Are" provides a written comment. The second document lists the statistics and ranking.

I hope this will be of assistance.

Yours sincerely,

Richard Coppin

Census Customer Services
Room 4300S

Northwick Park Road, Harrow, Middlesex

Mo Just
Chambers Dictionaries
Chambers Harrap Publishers Ltd
7 Hopetoun Crescent
Edinburgh
EH7 4AY

16th October 2002

Dear Mo

There seems to be a word missing.

I know that your excellent dictionary contains thousands upon thousands of words. But there is no entry for those little bits of dirty rubber left over when using an eraser. The word is, of course, screlchings.

Please can you let me know when this will be added to your next edition?

Kind regards

John Summers

CHAMBERS HARRAP Publishers Ltd

7 HOPETOUN CRESCENT, EDINBURGH EH7 4AY
TELEPHONE: 0131 556 5929   FAX: 0131 556 5313
E-MAIL: Admin@ChambersHarrap.co.uk

Mr John Summers
█ Northwick Park Road
Harrow
Middlesex
HA1 2NY

7 November, 2002

Dear Mr Summers,

New word

Thank you for your recent letter concerning *screlchings*. We are always grateful to receive suggestions for new words to add to our dictionaries. I am unable to find this word in any other source. Like other dictionary publishers, it is not our policy to include words until they have been used by a range of people over a reasonable period of time

Having said that, if people find these words useful, and start to repeat them, it is possible that they will catch on and eventually merit a place in the dictionary. Every new word that enters the dictionary has to start somewhere.

Thank you for your interest.

Yours sincerely,

Elaine O'Donoghue
Assistant Editor

Registered Office: 7 Hopetoun Crescent, Edinburgh EH7 4AY
Registered Company No. SC2048

The Old Rectory, Devon

The MD
Mars Confectionary
Dundee Rd
Slough
SL1 4JX

17th May 2006

Dear Sir / Madam

I'm glad to see that while you are the MD, your "Principle No1" states that I, as the consumer, am your boss.

Please can you settle the argument once and for all?

Precisely what size of Mars bar is required to fulfill the claim that "a Mars a day helps you work, rest and play"? You seem to have so many sizes, starting with the 'fun' size at 20g, then the snack bar at 38.5g, the lunchpack at 54g, the standard bar at 62.5g and finally, right at the top of the pile, the kingsize at 85g.

Presumably it all depends upon the size of the individual concerned? In that case I'm prepared to give you some personal information: I weigh 87kg. If you require any other biometric data before you give me an accurate answer, just let me know.

Perhaps can you send me a table that shows which size of bar is required by which weight / height / age of individual?

Also, please explain why the 20g bar is 'fun' but the larger ones are not?

Kind regards

John Summers

Masterfoods

A Division of Mars U.K. Limited

Freeby Lane
Waltham-on-the-Wolds
Melton Mowbray
Leicestershire LE14 4RS

Mr John Summers
The Old Rectory

26 May 2006   Our Ref: 37379350

Dear Mr Summers,

Thank you for contacting us regarding Mars.

The advertising phrase "a Mars a day helps you work rest and play" was based on the standard 62.5g bar.

As for the 20g bar being fun, we think all chocolate is fun and most enjoyable!

Thank you for taking the time to contact us. If you need any further information or advice please contact our Consumer Careline on the telephone number below and one of our Consumer Care Advisors will be more than happy to help you.

Yours sincerely

Margaret Henson
Consumer Care Team
0800 952 1234

Encs:

T+44 (0) 1664 410000 - F+44 (0) 1664 415661   www.mars.com

Registered at the Companies Registration Office: London, England - Registered number 636458
Registered Office: 3d Dundee Road, Slough SL1 4LG MASTERFOODS is a trademark

Northwick Park Road, Harrow, Middlesex

Mrs Lesley Lee
Consumer Services Manager
Polo Mints section
Nestlé UK Ltd
PO Box 203
York
YO91 1XY

27th September 2002

Dear Mrs Lee

Please can you settle the argument once and for all?

How many packets of Polo mints am I allowed to consume each week, without risking sterility? And what is the truth about whether excessive quantities of Polos make men go sterile?

Kind regards

John Summers

Nestlé UK Ltd

YORK YO91 1XY

TELEPHONE (01904) 604604
FACSIMILE (01904) 604534

www.nestle.co.uk

Mr John Summers
███ Northwick Park Road
HARROW
Middlesex
HA1 2NY

DIRECT LINE: 0800 000030

DIRECT FAX (01904) 603461

0962091A	1 October 2002	
YOUR REF.	OUR REF.	DATE

Dear Mr Summers

Thank you for your recent letter.

For some years information has been circulating that excessive eating of Polo Mints can lower the male virility. This is alarmist and misleading, and is not true. We can understand your concerns and would like to assure you that there is no ingredient in this product that can cause this problem.

We do not believe that there would be any danger in consuming an above average amount of Polo Mints always assuming that your diet as a whole is nutritious and that you do not have a weight problem.

Thank you once again for taking the trouble to contact us. I hope that this letter answers your concerns and that you will continue to enjoy our products in the future.

Yours sincerely

Mrs Debbie Edwards
Senior Supervisor
Consumer Services

The Old Rectory, Devon

The Big Red Button Pusher
London Traffic Control Centre
TfL Street Management
84 Eccleston Square
London
SW1V 1PX

12th June 2006

Dear Big Red Button Pusher

I am trying to find a career that uses my specialist skills. I have refined these by being hooked up to video games all day long. (And quite a lot of the night as well.)

I know that you have half a squillion VMS, CCTV and Enforcement cameras and loads and loads of screens and buttons to control them. Also I've heard that you have the power to move traffic jams around at will so that dignitaries, billionaires and Wayne Rooney can be whisked around London without being held up. How often do you push the 'Big Red Button' to sort this out?

Finally how can I put my skills, honed from playing video games, to use for the big capital?

Kind regards

John Summers

Transport for London

London Buses

BUSES

Our Ref: 372471/1/dp
Date: 03 August 2006

Mr John Summers
The Old Rectory

Devon

London Buses
Surface Transport
Customer Services

84 Eccleston Square
London SW1V 1PX

Phone 0845 300 7000
Fax 020 7027 9914
customerservices@tfl-buses.co.uk
www.tfl.gov.uk

Dear Mr Summers

Thank you for your recent letters regarding your interest in working for Transport for London, and road priority systems in London.

The closest system we can find to the one you mentioned is our Urban Traffic Control system (UTC). This is a dynamic new system which can really 'think for itself'. It can alter the timings of traffic lights automatically or we can change them via computer.

At UTC sites, we have detection systems, either on top of a signal head or on the ground at certain points along the roads adjoining the junction.

If there are stationary vehicles sitting over one of the ground detection systems, or in line with the ground detection systems, it will automatically increase the green time to reduce the waiting time to vehicles and clear the queue.

Meanwhile, if you would like to work for TfL, please see the following link to our careers website: http://www.tfl.gov.uk/tfl/jobs-introduction.asp

Thank you once again for taking the time to contact us. I wish you the very best of luck with your job hunting.

Yours sincerely

Daniel Palmer
Customer Services

London Bus Services Limited
trading as London Buses
whose registered office is as above.

Registered in England and Wales
Company number 3914787

VAT number 756 2770 08

London Bus Services Limited is a
company controlled by a local
authority within the meaning of
Part V Local Government and
Housing Act 1989. The controlling
authority is Transport for London.

BSI
REGISTERED
CMS 67818
London Buses Customer Services

POSITIVE ABOUT
DISABLED PEOPLE

MAYOR OF LONDON

The Old Rectory, Devon

Charlie Simpson
Fundraising Director
I CAN
4 Dyer's Building
Holborn
London
EC1N 2QP

31st October 2006

Dear Charlie

Would you like £10,000? Well the good news is that there's no catch, no small print, no "buy now, pay later" scam. It's a straightforward opportunity for I CAN to receive anything up to this amount. Really? Really.

I'm writing a book and, on the cover, I'd like to include a flash along the lines of "For each of the first 10,000 copies of this book sold, £1 will be donated to I CAN". So why have I chosen you?

While I don't have specific experience in the canning world, I have always had a keen interest in all aspects of packaging, crating and shrink-wrapping.

For instance, I know that we have to thank Napoleon for the concept of tinned food in 1809. On the other hand, what I don't know is the name of the person who wrote your official limerick. You know, the one that goes:

> There once was a canner so canny
> Who remarked with a smile to his granny
> "A canner can can
> Anything that he can
> But a canner can't can a can, can he?"

So, what do you think? Would you like to receive up to £10,000? In return, please let me know the name of your official poet. And can you consider me for professional membership of I CAN?

Kind regards

John Summers

**helps children
communicate**

REGISTERED CHARITY 210031

Mr John Summers
The Old Rectory

Devon

6th November 2006

Dear Mr Summers

Thank you very much for your letter dated 31 October.

Despite extensive research I am unable to reveal the poet behind the *Canny Canner*.
However, I would like to share with you a limerick I composed on the back of a bus ticket this
morning to highlight a major issue facing our education system today – poor language skills.

The new children started as planned,
Some with language skills way out of hand.
Helping them learn to read,
You might just concede,
Is like building a house on the sand.

Ok, I won't give up the day job quite yet, but the startling truth is that in deprived areas of the
UK, around 50% of children start school without the basic language skills they need to learn
and join-in.

1 in 10 have a specific communication disability, a problem processing language, which
means they struggle to understand what is said to them or find it hard to organise their
thoughts into meaningful speech. For many more children, their communication hasn't had
the support it needs to develop fully, leaving them with limited vocabularies, listening
difficulties, poor social skills and, often, unclear speech.

Unfortunately, what starts as a problem with speech and language early in life, all too often
leads to other significant problems later on. Links between behavioural and emotional
problems, low educational attainment, poor employment prospects and social exclusion are
both clear and strong.

As the charity that helps children communicate, we're immensely proud of our work, but
equally conscious that lots of children are not so lucky and don't get the right support. We
need to put our expertise and experience to work on a much greater scale.

I am therefore keen to find out more about you and your kind offer. Perhaps you could give
me a call and we can take it from there?

Thanks for your interest.

Yours sincerely,

Charlie Simpson
Deputy Director of Fundraising

I CAN is the children's communication charity.

I CAN, 8 Wakley Street, London EC1V 7QE Tel: 0845 225 4071 Fax: 0845 225 4072 E-mail: info@ican.org.uk www.ican.org.uk
Patron: HM The Queen • Founded in 1888 • Company Limited by Guarantee • Company Reg. No. 99629 (England & Wales)

The Old Rectory, Devon

Jonathan Ross
Friday Night With Jonathan Ross
Open Mike Productions
Hammer House
113-117 Wardour Street
London
W1F 0UN

19th December 2006

Dear Jonathan

You are a laugh! And have a great cavalier attitude to life. I love it.

Last week you had the wonderful Jimmy Carr on your programme. And you told us all how you have endorsed his book without even reading it. That's honesty for you!

Please can you do the same for me?

My book is called "Humps For 140 Yards". It aims to find answers to things we need to know. And, for the first 10,000 copies sold, I'll be giving £1 to children's communications charity I CAN (Registered Charity Number 210031).

So, how about agreeing to the following on the back cover:

"I've not actually read this book but John tells me it's a laugh." Jonathan Ross.

Alternatively, how about:

"I am unable to write anything about this book as I haven't read it." Jonathan Ross.

Kind regards

John Summers

Awaiting reply
but must go
to print...

Index